MARRIAGES

of

ROANE COUNTY,

TENNESSEE

1801 -1838

Marriages

of

Roane County, Tennessee

1801-1838

Compiled by
EDYTHE RUCKER WHITLEY

CLEARFIELD

Library of Congress Catalogue Card Number 83-81456

Reprinted for Clearfield Company by
Genealogical Publishing Company
Baltimore, Maryland
2011

ISBN 978-0-8063-1037-4

Made in the United States of America

Introduction

N NOVEMBER 30, 1793 a blockhouse was completed by John Sevier at Southwest Point, a station established two years earlier near present-day Kingston which was of great service to travelers and settlers as protection against the Indians. In 1799 the Tennessee Legislature, then in session in Knoxville, passed an act "To establish a town to be named Kingston, on the lands of Robert King, near Southwest Point, in Knox County, to be laid out under the direction of David Miller, Alexander Carmichael, George Preston, John Smith, William L. Lovely, and Thomas N. Clark." Later a petition was sent to the Legislature to create a new county with Kingston as the county seat. This was effected on November 6, 1801, when Roane County was formally erected from Knox County.

Until now the early marriage records of Roane County have not been fully published; even Emma M. Wells' *History of Roane County, Tennessee, 1801-1870,* which is an excellent publication, falls somewhat short of recording all the marriages that took place in the county in the early days. There are, possibly, a few records I have missed in this publication which were taken from the files in the courthouse and never returned, but I believe this is an almost complete record of the early marriages of the county.

The reader will note that *HRC* at the end of an entry indicates that the information was taken from Wells' *History,* and that the letters *CA* refer to the original bonds and licenses on file at the Roane County Courthouse in Kingston. With regard to the latter, the reader should note further that the first date given in each entry is the date of issue of the marriage bond or license. The date following (in parentheses) is the date the marriage was performed. If no date of marriage is given, then the single date provided refers merely to the date of issue of the marriage bond and does not *prove* that a marriage actually took place. The abbreviation *BM* signifies bondsman—one who affirms, by standing security, that there is no lawful cause to obstruct the marriage.

Edythe Rucker Whitley
Nashville, Tennessee

ROANE COUNTY, TENNESSEE

Marriages, 1801-1838

1801

John Powell to Ann Carter, Dec. 22, 1801.
  Micajah Carter, BM. (HRC)

1802

Robert Burk to Rebeccah Horton, Dec. 9, 1802.
  Henry Breaseale, BM. (CA)
Joshua Christenberry to Delilah Hanson, Sep. 2, 1802.
  (CA)
John Condon to Elizabeth Luster, Sep. 4, 1802.
  See also John Condon, 1805. (CA)
John Condon to Elizabeth Wester, Sep. 4, 1802.
  See also John Condon, 1805. (HRC)
William Davis to Betsey Roberts, Mar. 27, 1802.
  James Hankins, BM. (CA, HRC)
James Dearmond to Sucky Shadden, Mar. 15, 1802.
  Abraham McClellan, BM. (CA)
James Forrester to Polly Hankins, Jan. 2, 1802.
  (HRC)

1

Joseph Harker to Prissilla Haggerty, June 8, 1802.
John Thomas, BM. See also Joseph Walker, 1802. (CA)
John Hunt to Easter Bartly, Nov. 6, 1802.
William Sherrill, BM. (CA)
Benjamin Lively to Fanny Starke, Feb. 12, 1802.
Wright Roberts, BM. (CA)
John Lowery to Jane Scott, Mar. 24, 1802.
Bartly McGhee, BM. (CA)
William Luster to Rebecca Sims, Mar. 15, 1802.
Jacob Sims, Edward _____, BM. (HRC)
John McCord to Betsey Sharkey, July 10, 1802.
(HRC)
John McKinney to Mary Coleman, Sep. 25, 1802.
William McKinney, Wm. Caldwell, BM. (CA)
John Wear to Mary Burns, Oct. 25, 1802.
Hugh Wear, BM. (HRC)
John Mitchell to Winney Sullivan, Jan. 22, 1802.
James Mitchell, BM. (CA)
Edward Sweny to Nancy Eldridge, Aug. 27, 1802.
(CA)
Joseph Walker to Priscilla Haggerty, June 8, 1802.
John Thomas, BM. See also Joseph Harker, 1802.
(CA, HRC)
Samuel Williams to Nancy Harkins, June 22, 1802.
Alex Carmichael, BM (CA) James Haskins, BM (HRC)

1803

Charles Beckett to Lydda Holland, Mar. 5, 1803.
Ephraim Walker, BM. (CA)
William Blair to Sally Summers, Dec. 18, 1803.
Sampson Eldridge, BM. (CA)
William Campbell to Peggy Luttrell, Sep. 24, 1803.
David Stewart, BM. (CA)
Alexander Cassey to Mary Cooper, May 30, 1803.
Thomas Brown, BM. (CA)
Samuel Eldridge to Zylphey Tarbour, June 9, 1803.
Jared Hotchkiss, BM. (CA)
John Flat to Peggy Parker, Dec. 14, 1803.
(CA)
William Gallaher to Sally Davidson, Jan. 21, 1803.
Alexander Carmichal, Alexander Hopkins, BM. (CA)
John Gambell to Betsey Evine, July 12, 1803.
James Gallaher, BM. (HRC)
William Gardenhire to Ann Rogers Rather, Oct. 12, 1803.
William Rather, BM. (CA)
Thomas Gormany to Becky Avery, Aug. 4, 1803.
Peter Avery, BM. (CA)
Alexander Hines to Polly Sharky, Feb. 4, 1803.
Alexander Carmichael, William Miller, BM. (CA)
William Matlock to Sally Walker, Jan. 4, 1803.
Ephraim Walker, BM. (HRC)
John Miller to Mary Wear, Mar. 4, 1803.
Wm. Barnett, BM. (CA)

ROANE COUNTY MARRIAGES

Thomas Stafford to Rosey Baskin, Nov. 11, 1803.
(CA)
Augustus Strong to Louisa Shephard, Apr. 4, 1803.
Townley Deakins, Thomas Oliver, BM. (HRC)
Martin Thomas to Nancy Callison, Oct. 25, 1803.
Thomas Fulton, BM. (CA)
William Willett to Mary Fagan, Mar. 22, 1803.
Jas. Willett, BM. (CA)
Jonathan Williams to Rachel Roberts, ___ 27, 1803.
(CA)

1804

Isaac Bailey to Betsey Marney, Apr. 13, 1804.
(CA)
Thomas Bozeman to Amy Miller, July 24, 1804.
Alex Miller, BM. (CA)
William Car to Margaret _____, Apr. 18, 1804.
Hugh Beatty, M. A. Allison, BM. (CA)
William Car to Peggy Brown, Apr. 14, 1804.
(CA)
Townley Deakins to Agness Rentfroe, Feb. 11, 1804.
(CA)
Daniel Durne to Sarah Stone, Mar. 19, 1804.
Edward Walker, BM. (HRC)
Woodson Francis to Betsy Thomas, Apr. 19, 1804.
Joseph Hankins, BM. (CA)
John Freeman to Sucky Davis, Jan. 28, 1804.
Bazzil Davis, BM. (CA)
John Hughes to Mary Nelson, June 22, 1804.
Ephraim Walker, BM. (CA)
William Johnson to Matty Rogers, Sep. 7, 1804.
Gains Johnson, BM. (CA)
Robert Mahan to Patsy Sherrell, Aug. 4, 1804.
Alexander Mahan, BM. (CA)
James McKain to Ginnet Sims, July 4, 1804.
Matthew Sims, BM. (CA)
Thomas McKinney to Jean Sharp, July 23, 1804.
William McKinney, David Moore, BM. (CA)
John McNairy to Nancy Riley, May 9, 1804.
Samuel Riley, Jesse Byrd, BM. (CA)
William Morgan to Peggy Walker, Feb. 18, 1804.
James Morris, BM. (CA)
William Prewitt to Sally Cavett, Nov. 29, 1804.
(CA)
Samuel S. Bankin to Mary White, Sep. 1, 1804.
(CA)
John Rogers to Elizabeth Coody, Apr. 4, 1804.
Hugh Beatty, Townley Deakins, BM. (CA)
John Walker to Ginny Galloway, Mar. 9, 1804.
James Galloway, BM. (CA)
Hugh White to Mary Johnson, Feb. 9, 1804.
William Barnett, BM. (HRC)

3

Thomas Bibe to Polly Roach, July 4, 1805.
Ansley Roach, BM. (CA)
James Breazeale to Peggy Miller, Aug. 8, 1805.
Thomas Pritchett, BM. (CA)
John Brown to Polly Allison, July 12, 1805.
Henry Breazeale, BM. (CA)
William Brown to Stacey Grason, Oct. 28, 1805.
(HRC)
Jesse Byrd to Catherine Taylor, Jan. 7, 1805.
Little Page Sims, BM. (CA)
John Cery to Susanah Hawkins, Jan. __, 1805.
Richard Oliver, BM. See also John Essery, 1805. (CA)
John Condon to Elizabeth Luster, Sep. 4, 1805.
See also John Condon, 1802. (CA)
James Craige to Amy Allison, May 20, 1805.
Uriah Allison, BM. (CA)
Simpson Eldridge to Fannie Simmons, Aug. 20, 1805.
Jesse Eldridge, BM. (HRC)
John Essery to Susanah Hawkins, Jan. __, 1805.
Daniel Hare, BM. See also John Cery, 1805. (HRC)
Thomas Gallbreath to Peggy White, Jan. 14, 1805.
William White, BM. (CA)
Jeremiah Henson to Fanny Abels, Aug. 16, 1805.
(CA)
Jeremiah Hynson to Fanny Lyles, Aug. 16, 1805.
Jesse Delozier, Isaac Shinalt, BM. No return. Issued
in 1805 and 1807. (CA)
James James to Nancy Givens, Nov. 8, 1805.
Enid Waller, BM. (CA)
John Johnson to Lyda Coupland, July 20, 1805.
William Holland, BM. (CA)
Thomas Lay to Sarah Smith, Sep. 16, 1805.
Daniel Hare, BM. (HRC)
James Luster to Amy Jones, Nov. 16, 1805.
John Luster, David Lee, BM. (CA)
Alex Mahan to Ruthy Henley, Mar. 20, 1805.
(CA)
David Maloney to Ginny Christenberry, Jan. 25, 1805.
James Crouch, BM. (CA)
Abraham McClellan to Juliana Toomy, Aug. 20, 1805.
James Toomy, BM. (CA)
John McElwee to Patsey True, Dec. 26, 1805.
Isham Cox, BM. (CA)
Francis Miller to Mary Findley, Sep. 25, 1805.
James Miller, BM. (HRC)
Richard Oliver to Elizabeth Allen, Nov. 30, 1805.
J. W. Wood, BM. (CA)
John Prater to Peggy Wood, Dec. 28, 1805.
John Wood, BM. (HRC)
Moses Raskins to Caty Allison, Sep. 16, 1805.
(CA)
John Simpson to Pheby Mahan, Mar. 11, 1805.
Alexander Mahan, BM. (CA)

Thomas Upton to Emmey Wilson, June 20, 1805.
  John Brown, Mark Renfroe, BM. (HRC)
Jacob Work to Sera (Sarah?) Willett, Aug. 26, 1805.
  James Willett, BM. (CA)

1806

Wm. C. Allen to Mary Wright, Dec. 27, 1806.
  George W. Wheat, BM. (CA)
Daniel Brown to Janes Ellender, Feb. 2, 1806.
  Robert Noble, BM. (CA)
John Buford to Nancy Johnson, Apr. 24, 1806.
  Thomas Johnson, BM. (CA)
David Collier to Rhoda Minnis, Oct. 12, 1806.
  Hugh Francis, BM. (CA)
Richard Cooper to Mary McCoy, A.D. 1806.
  Zacheus Ayers, James McNutt, BM. (CA)
Isaac Councill to Susanah Allison, Apr. 14, 1806.
  (CA)
Samuel Dudley to Mattie Sherold, Aug. 19, 1806.
  Jesse Sherold, BM. (CA)
Phillip Foshall to Betsey Robinett, Feb. 26, 1806.
  James Mitchell, BM. (CA)
Jesse Goodwin to Caty Coulter, June 16, 1806.
  John Coulter, BM. (CA)
George Hitchcoke to Milly Riddle, Mar. 11, 1806.
  Elizabeth Hitchcoke, BM. (CA)
William Lee to Elizabeth Means, Jan. 21, 1806.
  Stephen Morris, BM. (CA)
Royal Matlock to Nancy Mahan, Sep. 3, 1806.
  James Roberts, BM. (CA)
James McCullough to Rebecky Pruett, Jan. 8, 1806.
  Bazel Brashear, BM. (CA)
Daniel McDaniel to Sally Smith, Mar. 17, 1806.
  Lem White, BM. (CA)
William McNutt to Mary Blackwell, Oct. 13, 1806.
  Azariah David, Owen David, BM. (CA)
Nathan Melton to Peggy Kerns, Mar. 15, 1806.
  Milton Center, BM. (CA)
Morris Moore to Dianah Adams, Nov. 6, 1806.
  Thomas Moore, James Nail, BM. (HRC)
John Poulston to Samuel McKinny, Jan. 25, 1806.
  Benjamin Flatt, BM. (CA)
Elisha Randolph to Polly Evans, Nov. 18, 1806.
  Benjamin Evans, BM. (CA)
William Richards to Polly Phillips, Aug. 10, 1806.
  Joel Holt, BM. (HRC)
James Roberts to Delilah Woods, June 10, 1806.
  Joseph Hankins, BM. (HRC)
Samuel Roberts to Deliah Woods, June 16, 1806.
  Joseph Hankins, BM. (CA)
William Rorax to Polly Keys, Jan. 14, 1806.
  Samuel Keys, BM. (CA)
Thomas Safford to Rosey Baskin, Nov. 22, 1806.
  Frances Fulcher, BM. (HRC)

Jesse Sherrell to Polly Francis, Feb. 6, 1806.
  Hugh Francis, BM. (CA)
Noah Stafford to Sally Blackwell, Nov. 5, 1806.
  John Dixon, Martin Nelson, BM. (CA)
Zacheus Tooten to Ally Dixon, Aug. 4, 1806.
  Martin Nelson, William McNutt, BM. (CA)
Edward Waller to Mariah Duncan, Nov. 15, 1806.
  James McNutt, BM. (CA)
Thomas Whitworth to Sarah Eblen, July 19, 1806.
  James Thomas, BM. (CA)
William Wilson to <u>Chainey</u> Hornsby, Dec. 8, 1806.
  William Parker, Garnet Hornsby, BM. (Dec. 8, 1806) (CA)

1807

John Allen to Alice Oliver, Dec. 30, 1807.
  John Preston, BM. (CA)
William Ballard to Polly Eblen, May 22, 1807.
  Hugh Frances, BM. (HRC)
Peter Berry to Rebecca Buchanan, Feb. 24 (or 25), 1807.
  (CA, HRC)
William Bigham to Lyda Gragg, Dec. 14, 1807.
  John Ellis, BM. (CA)
William Brown to Sally Kimbrough, Mar. 20, 1807.
  (CA)
Ambrose Bryant to Polly Toomy, Nov. 13, 1807.
  Preston Hickey, Samuel Woody, BM. (CA)
Phillip Burch to Polly Paine, May 23, 1807.
  Abraham Shafer, BM. (HRC)
William Burgis to Mary Man, Aug. 5, 1807.
  Edward Springston, BM. (CA)
John Casteel to Janey Lane, Sep. 23, 1807.
  Robert Lane, BM. (CA)
George Crow to Sally White, June 21, 1807.
  William White, BM. (CA)
David Dean to Gracey Joiner, Nov. 27 (or 24), 1807.
  William Joiner, BM. (HRC)
John Derick to Caty Bird. Dec. 7, 1807.
  George Derick, Henry Derick, BM. (HRC)
William Eblen to Patsey Galloway, May 3, 1807.
  Stephen Morris, BM. (CA)
Jeremiah Hynson to Fannie Lyles, Aug 6, <u>1807</u>.
  Isaac Shualt, Robert Lyles, BM. (HRC)
Peter Holland to Polly Lea, Jan. 19, 1807.
  (CA)
John Husk to Nancy Thompson, July 14, 1807.
  James Thompson, BM. (CA)
William Johnson to Polly Davis, June 26, 1807.
  Richard A. Cooper, BM. (June <u>24</u>, 1807) (CA)
David Lea to Judith Davis, May <u>11</u>, 1807.
  John Formwalt, BM. (CA)
William L. Lovely to Mrs. Persis Goodrich, Feb. 15, 1807.
  Samuel Riley, BM. Emigrated to Arkansas, 1812.
  (CA, HRC)

William Lyon to Polly Clark, Sep. 10, 1807.
Samuel C. Hall, BM. (CA)
Jason Matlock to Polly Miller, Nov. 24, 1807.
Robert Burk, BM. (CA)
Francis Miller to Hannah Henry, Apr. 26, 1807.
Ezekiel Henry, BM. (CA)
John Miller to Jenny Stubb, Nov. 9, 1807.
Jason Matlock, BM. (CA)
Hall Richard to Marian Prewitt, Sep. 4, 1807.
Michael Hostler, BM. (CA)
Daniel Self to Ann Robinson, Jan. 3, 1807.
John Jones, BM. (CA, HRC)
Henry Self to Betsey Owen, Mar. 26, 1807.
Levi Self, Mathew Nelson, BM. (CA)
Henry Self to Betsey Allin, Mar. 7, 1807.
Levi Self, Mathew Nelson, BM. (HRC)
Michael Straisner to Elizabeth Brashears, Apr. 20, 1807.
Zaza Brashears, BM. (CA)
Charles Sweazea to Elizabeth Jones, Feb. 9, 1807.
Richard Sweazea, BM. (CA)
Martin Thomas to Eliza M. Stinson, June 20, 1807.
Richard Oliver, BM. (CA)
Wiley Tuten to Rachel Cody, June 6, 1807.
John Riley, Absolum Dixon, BM. (HRC)
John Walker to Caty Stone, Jan. 17, 1807.
Daniel Mason, BM. (Jan. 17, 1807) (CA)
John Wearing to Lyda May, July 30, 1807.
William Brown, BM. (CA)
Samuel Wilkerson to Betsey Brashears, Mar. 19, 1807.
Jesse Sherrell, BM. (CA)

1808

Elias Allen to Sally Holly, Oct. 3, 1808.
Jonathan Harvey, BM. (CA)
Moses Archer to Sally Moore, Jan. 9, 1808.
(CA)
Robert Bashears to Sallie Hankins (no date given).
James Hankins, Betsy Puris, BM. (HRC)
Richard Bower to Patsey Derrett, June 21, 1808.
William Derrett, BM. (CA)
Samuel Bradley to Peggy Taylor, Sep. 8 (or 28), 1808.
Little Page Sims, BM. (CA, HRC)
Robert Brashears to Sally Hankins, Nov. 19, 1808.
James Hankins, BM. (CA)
Zaza Brashears to Polly Rice, Mar. 25, 1808.
John B. Rice, BM. (CA)
William Burris to Elizabeth Wilson, Feb. 14, 1808.
John McEwin, Jeremiah Buchanan, Wm. Wilson, BM. (CA)
George Delozier to Penina Rowden, Jan. 2, 1808.
Willis Breazeale, BM. (CA)
Elijah Dixon to Rebecca Oden, July 15, 1808.
Samuel Waddy, BM. (CA)
Benjamin Draper to Nancy Sweza, May 7, 1808.
(CA)

Elijah Evans to Nancy Fouche, July 12, 1808.
Henry Breazeale, BM. (HRC)
Mathew Griffith to Nancy Holloway, Aug. 31, 1808.
Thomas Griffith, BM. (CA)
William Harvey to Rhoda Rogers, Dec. 13, 1808.
Asa Richards, BM. (CA)
Henry Haynes to Lucinda Neal, Aug. 23, 1808.
Abner Majors, BM. See also Henry Hines, 1808. (HRC)
George W. Henson to Polly Gardner, Oct. 3, 1808.
Ephraim Pritchett, BM. (CA)
Henry Hines to Lucinda Nail, Aug. 22, 1808.
Abney Majors, BM. See also Henry Haynes. (CA)
William Holland to Polly Short, April 9, 1808.
Abraham K. Shafer, BM. (Apr. 9, 1808) (CA)
Morgan Hood to Winefred Self, Spe. 12, 1808.
Daniel Self, BM. (CA)
Lark Julias to Elizabeth McDonald, June 11, 1808.
Nathaniel Cox, BM. (CA)
Samuel Kees (or Keys) to Polly Riley, Apr. 2, 1808.
Gilbert Pool, BM. (HRC)
Edward Kirpatrick to Polly Jones, Oct. 18, 1808.
Lewis Kirkpatrick, BM. (CA)
Daniel Little to Polly Tummins, Nov. 11, 1808.
Samuel Tummins, BM. (HRC)
David McGill to Polly McCrary, Oct. 19, 1808.
James McGill, BM. (CA)
John McKamy to Finney Letterson Walker, Oct. 13, 1808.
Samuel Walker, Daniel McClellan, BM. (CA)
Alexander McKinney to Priscilla Lyle, Sep. 5, 1808.
David Webb, BM. (CA)
James McMullin to Rebecca McMullin, Feb. 1, 1808.
Samuel McMullin, BM. (CA)
James Nail to Elizabeth Hopkins, June 25, 1808.
Mathew Nail, BM. (CA)
James Noble to Penny Hoffner, June 21, 1808.
Thos. Griffith, BM. (June 21, 1808) (CA)
Mathew Prior to Henrietta Williams, Sep. 22, 1808.
Josiah Gent, BM. (CA)
John Rather to Nancy Nail, May 8, 1808.
(May 8, 1817?) (CA)
Bartlett Robin to Caty McNutt, Sep. 8, 1808.
Samuel Waddy, BM. (CA, HRC)
James Sappington to Polly Dickson, Oct. 8, 1808.
Absolom Dickson, Martin Nelson, BM. (CA)
Sanders Sisco to Betsey Baker, Apr. 27, 1808.
Nathaniel Cox, BM. (CA)
James Trimble to Letitia Lyon, Nov. 10, 1808.
William Lyon, Richard H. Love, BM. (CA)
George Vaughn to Caty Roberts, Mar. 26, 1808.
(Mar. 26, 1808) (CA)
Robert White to Ann Austen, Dec. 27, 1808.
John White, BM. (CA)
Lewis Widener to Anna Click, Jan. 7, 1808.
Peter Wingener, BM. (HRC)

Stephen Wright to Jennie Buchanan, Nov. 13, 1808.
Samuel Stout, BM. (CA)

1809

William Adair to Nancy Rather, Nov. 18, 1809.
Samuel Riley, BM. (HRC)
Russell Alexander to Betsey Rice, Nov. 16, 1809.
Mathew Nelson, BM. (CA)
Elias Allen to Sally Holly, Oct. 3, 1809.
(HRC)
James Beavers to Betsy Forshee, May 27, 1809.
Azariah Cooper, BM. (HRC)
Abner Casey to Polly Ellison, Sep. 30, 1809.
John Dotson, BM. (CA)
Jonathan Clenny to Jinny Husett, Oct. 20, 1809.
John Dirgin, BM. (HRC)
Adam Crag to Betsey Pryor, Apr. 21, 1809.
James Robinson, BM. (CA)
Thomas Craig to Peggy Stonecipher, Oct. 11, 1809.
Andrew Pruitt, BM. (HRC)
Hugh Crumbliss to Betsey Brashears, Aug. 27, 1809.
Isaac Brashears, BM. (CA)
Llea Dosset to Polly Holland, Nov. 10, 1809.
Joshua Burdwell, BM. (CA)
Absolom Eakins to June (or Jane) Sutton, Dec. 26, 1809.
Thomas Blackston, BM. (CA, HRC)
Israel Gable to Kitty Reid, Feb. 3, 1809.
John Thornton, BM. (CA)
John Gillispie to Nancy Gallaher, Mar. 13, 1809.
Mathew Donald (or Mathew Donaldson), BM. (CA, HRC)
Jas. Green to Susanah Rouden, Nov. 3 (or 23), 1809.
Echols Rouden (or Ekale Rowden), BM. (Nov. 23, 1809)
(CA, HRC)
Julius Hacker to Sarah Hagerty, Oct. 29, 1809.
Samuel McCall, BM. (CA)
Thomas Harvey to Rachel Carter, Sep. 27, 1809.
Edward Eblen, BM. (HRC)
Preston Hickey to Elizabeth Barnett, Aug. 2, 1809.
Alexander Forbish, BM. (CA)
David Dalb to Esther Pellum, Aug. 24, 1809.
Jesse Pellum, BM. (CA)
John Kennedy (or Kenneley) to Eady Dunlap, Mar. 13 (or
14), 1809. Abraham K. Shafer, BM. (March 13, 1809)
(CA, HRC)
Robert King to Milly Morgan, Sep. 19, 1809.
Samuel Thacker, BM. (CA)
Alpha Kingsley (or Kinsley) to Eliza Ayers (or Ayer),
Nov. 15, 1809. Ephraim Pritchett, BM. (CA)
James McClintock to Elizabeth Langford, Feb. 9, 1809.
Noah Ashley, BM. (CA)
George Moore to Polly Simmons, June 24, 1809.
Mordicia Mitchell, BM. (CA)
Thomas Moore to Polly Kindrick, Dec. 25, 1809.
Benjamin Moore, BM. (CA, HRC)

John Neal to Ellender Harrison, Mar. 13, 1809.
  William Thomas, BM. (HRC)
John Nichols to Sally Sharp, July 25, 1809.
  Samuel Stout, BM. (CA)
John Parker to Eliza Stover, Oct. 26, 1809.
  David Warding, BM. (CA)
William Parker to Cilly Barnett, Nov. 17, 1809.
  David Warden, BM. (CA)
David Patton to Betsy Purris, Jan. 24, 1809.
  John Purris, BM. (HRC)
John Riley to Suckie Walker (Cherokees), Jan. 25, 1809.
  Gilbert Pool, BM. (HRC)
Christopher Robinson to Sally Rector, Mar. 6, 1809.
  Lewis Robinson, Abraham Shaifer, BM. (HRC)
David Scrivner to Susanah Bowman, Oct. 28, 1809.
  Noah Ashley, BM. (CA)
George Smith to Mary Atmer(?), Nov. 25, 1809.
  Stephen Wright, BM. (CA)
George Stephens to Polly Moore, Apr. 19, 1809.
  (CA)
James Tippett to Catesey(?) Ramsey, Dec. 30, 1809.
  Samuel McCall, BM. (CA)
Buckner Walker to Peggy McCain, Mar. 17, 1809.
  James Hope, BM. (CA)
John Webb to Nancy Hall, Aug. 4, 1809.
  Martin Hall, BM. (CA)
Samuel Wilkerson to Jinny McComb, May 6, 1809.
  Isaac Gibson, BM. (CA)
Caleb Wood to Polly Oliver, June 7, 1809.
  James Matlock, BM. (CA)
Stephen Wright to Jeminia Buchanan, Nov. 13, 1809.
  Samuel Stout, BM. (HRC)

1810

James Bailey to Polly Rector, Feb. 17, 1810.
  John Rector, BM. (HRC)
Isaac Bullar to Sally Geren, Jan. 24, 1810.
  Samuel Geren, Daniel Kirkpatrick, BM. (CA, HRC)
Charlie Burk to Nancy Bowman, Nov. 2, 1810.
  John Bowman, BM. (HRC)
Charles Coodey to Elenor Riley, Aug. 18, 1810.
  John Oden, BM. (HRC)
Hugh Crumbliss to Betsy Bashears, Aug. 27, 1810.
  Isaac Brashears, BM. (HRC)
James Eddington to Phebe Butler, Sep. 14, 1810.
  Peter Click, BM. (CA)
Benjamin Evans to Betsy K. Moore, Sep. 4, 1810.
  Wm. McKamy, BM. (CA)
Alexander Galbreath to Polly Gallaher, Sep. 3, 1810.
  James Gallaher, BM. (HRC)
Joseph Hacker to Priscilla Haggerty, July 14, 1810.
  William Small, BM. (CA)
John Haggart to Sarah Smith, Apr. 7, 1810.
  James Haggart, John Smith, BM. (HRC)

James Haggert to Jenny Drinkard, Feb. 16, 1810.
John Draper, BM. (CA)
John Hart to Ruth Stout, Oct. 1, 1810.
James Dearmond, BM. (HRC)
Robert Hewett to Rebecca Phillips, Mar. 13, 1810.
James Robinson, BM. (HRC)
Calvin Johnson to Nancy McKamey, Dec. 10, 1810.
William McKaney, BM. (HRC)
Isaac Keys to Elizabeth Riley, Aug. 21, 1810.
Gilbert Pool, BM. (CA)
Tandy Lane to Mary Jones, Sep. 18, 1810.
Benjamin Prater, BM. (CA)
Mason Luttrell to Elizabeth Eldridge, Jan. 24, 1810.
Edward Luttrell, BM. (CA)
Amos Marney to Patsey Young, May 1, 1810.
Isham Young, BM. (CA)
James Massey to Susana Lee, June 9, 1810.
James Morrow, Jacob Work, BM. (CA)
Moore Matlock to Lucy Knight, July 4, 1810.
William Anderson, BM. (HRC)
Henry Miller to Polly Erwin, Feb. 15, 1810.
James Breazeale, BM. (CA)
Thomas Moore to Anna Maria Greer, Jan. 6, 1810.
Benjamin Moore, BM. (CA)
John Morgan to Jenny Kain, Jan. 3, 1810.
John Hood, BM. (CA)
John Moton to Jenny Kelly, Feb. 5, 1810.
(HRC)
Samuel Nipp to Elizabeth Riley, Aug. 16, 1810.
Charles Cody, John Odin, BM. (HRC)
William Oliver to Peggy Lacefield, June 10 (or Jan. 12),
1810. John Allen, BM. (CA, HRC)
John Panky to Peggy Owen, Aug. 20, 1810.
Drewy Smith, BM. (CA)
Jesse Pellum to Peggy Culp, Feb. 16, 1810.
Mathew Wood, BM. (Feb. 16, 1810) (CA, HRC)
William Pellum to Patty World, Feb. 23, 1810.
William Winegar, BM. (CA)
Reuben Phillips to Kitty Bowers, Dec. 22, 1810.
James Robinson, BM. (HRC)
James Preston to Jinny Allison, Nov. 7, 1810.
Uriah Allison, BM. (HRC)
Wiley Walker to Patsey Robertson, Jan. 19, 1810.
Charles Coady, BM. (Jan. 19, 1810) (CA, HRC)
Jacob Warren to Betsey Elkins, Oct. 5, 1810.
John Hankins, BM. (CA)
James Warren to Nancy Evans, Feb. 23, 1810.
Arden Evans, BM. (HRC)
Elisha Williamson to Sally Matlock, May 20 (or 25), 1810.
James Matlock, BM (CA, HRC)

1811

Thomas Anderson to Patsey Essery, Sep. 18, 1811.
Adam Carson, BM. (CA)

John Black to Peggy Eldridge, Mar. 8, 1811.
William Gardenhire, BM. (CA)
James Bowman to Rachel McCorkle, Oct. 1, 1811.
Hugh Francis, BM. (CA)
John Brazil to Rhoda Stonecypher, July 15, 1811.
(CA)
Enoch Connelly to Ann Couch, Oct. 1, 1811.
(CA)
Robert Crawford to Susanna Brown, Aug. 27, 1811.
(CA)
John Dauret to Elizabeth Coatney, Dec. 7, 1811.
John Doss, BM. See also John Gaunt, 1811. (HRC)
Alfred Davis to Betsy Breazeale, Nov. 25, 1811.
William Haskins, BM. (HRC)
Jeremiah Evans to Sally Davis, Nov. 6, 1811.
Little B. Bryant, BM. (CA)
John Gaunt to Elizabeth Coatney, Dec. 7, 1811.
William Coatney, BM. See also John Dauret, 1811. (CA)
John Givens to Louis Stubbs, Jan. 22, 1811.
Hugh Francis, BM. (CA)
Samuel Haggard to Elizabeth Montgomery, Dec. 24, 1811.
(CA)
Gilbert Hankins to Polly Pippins, Sep. 9, 1811.
John Loyd, BM. (CA)
James Hankins to Lucinda England, Oct. 4, 1811.
Jeremiah Fields, BM. (CA)
William Hankins to Nancy Davis, May 31, 1811.
James McMullin, BM. (CA)
Daniel Hastler to Nancy Noel, July 16, 1811.
David Thomas, BM. (HRC)
Charles Hickey to Lucinda England, Oct. 4, 1811.
Jeremiah Fielder, BM. (HRC)
John Jackson to Polly Preston, May 26, 1811.
John Harrison, BM. (CA)
Reuben McKinnie to Jenny Lyle, Sep. 6, 1811.
Robert Lyle, BM. (HRC)
James McMullin to Rebeccka Miller, Oct. 31, 1811.
William Eblen, BM. (CA)
James McNair to Rebecka Walker, July 2, 1811.
Augustus McKinney, BM. (July 2, 1811) (CA)
John Mead to Elizabeth Matlock, July 9, 1811.
Joshua Cox, BM. (CA)
William Pennalan to Mary Casey, June 29, 1811.
Abner Casey, Abrahan Stout, BM. See also William
Pimerlore, 1811. (CA)
Jacob Perrygin to Betsey Mund, Sep. 12, 1811.
_____ Harrison, BM. (CA)
Clemmens Philips to Drusilla Prewett, July 16, 1811.
John W. Bowers, BM. (CA)
William Pimerlore to Mary Corey, June 29, 1811.
See also William Pennalan. (HRC)
Alexander Powell to Patsey Browder, Sep. 11 (or 17), 1811.
Brittain Mathews, BM. (CA, HRC)
James Renfro to Sally Lyle, Feb. 1, 1811.
James Buchanan, John Loyd, BM. (CA)

Thomas Richardson to Elizabeth Ellison, Aug. 1, 1811.
  Ambler Casey, BM. (HRC)
James Rogers to Nancy Coady, May 11 (or 26), 1811.
  Wiley Tuton, BM. (CA, HRC)
Etheldrid Taylor to Catherine H. Arbuckle, Dec. 11, 1811.
  Wm. Brown, BM. (HRC)
John Thacker to Nellie Brazelton, Aug. 28, 1811.
  James Hunt, BM. (HRC)
Joseph Thompson to Polly Hopkins, Sep. 11, 1811.
  (HRC)
Ruban Tiner to Jinney Carter, Dec. 3, 1811.
  (CA)
Daniel Turner to Betsey Hill, Oct. 18, 1811.
  (CA)
Abner Waters to Betsey Rayburn, Oct. 5 (or 11), 1811.
  Samuel Stout, BM. (CA, HRC)
John Watson to Jinny Kelly, Feb. 5, 1811.
  William Dunlap, BM. (CA)
Charles White to Nancy McPherson, Apr. 26, 1811.
  Barton McPherson, BM. (CA)
George White to Hannah McPherson, May 15, 1811.
  (CA)

1812

John Avery to Betsey Letihworth, Dec. 15, 1812.
  Peter Avery, BM. (CA)
Samuel Bazil to Eliza Scott, May 5, 1812.
  Samuel Williams, BM. (CA)
Wm. Beeman to Susanna Buchannan, Aug. 26, 1812.
  Jeremiah Buchanan, BM. (CA)
David Breaseale to Rosey Matlock, Jan. 22, 1812.
  John Matlock, Woods Breazeale, BM. (CA)
Samuel Breazeale to Eliza Scott, Jan. 22, 1812.
Ab'm Bogart to Jinny Preston, July 12, 1812.
  James Burk, BM. (CA)
William Bogart to Jenny Preston, Jan. 4, 1812.
  James Preston, BM. No return. (CA)
Ephraim Bridges to Betsy White, Mar. 25, 1812.
  Benjamin Shields, BM. (HRC)
Joseph Browder to Nancy Eldridge, Mar. 24, 1812.
  Brittain Mathews, BM. (CA)
Moses Cavett to Polly Pickle, Feb. 26, 1812.
  (HRC)
James Davis to Nancy Woods, Dec. 19, 1812.
  Asa Cobb, BM. (CA)
Richard Dover to Dice Rice, July 13, 1812.
  James Rice, BM. (CA)
Berry Duncan to Fanny Tummins, July 16, 1812.
  Isaac McMeans, BM. (CA)
John England to Lennie Hall, May 26, 1812.
  Squire Hendrix, BM. (CA)
Thomas Fields to Lusy Holly, Feb. 29, 1812.
  (CA)

Joseph Hankins to Betsey Irvin, Mar. 11, 1812.
John Essery, BM. (Mar. 11, 1812) (CA)
Samuel Hope to Agnes Duncan, Oct. 6 (or 16), 1812.
Jeptha Duncan, BM. (CA, HRC)
William Kelly to Ruth Prigmore, Jan 7 (or 27), 1812.
James May, BM. (CA, HRC)
Silas Luttrell to Stacey Burnett, Sep. 7, 1812.
Moses Burnett, BM. (CA)
Oliver Morris to Katy Eldridge, Oct. 24, 1812.
James Cozby, BM. (CA)
John Oden to Eliza Eblen, June 6, 1812.
(CA)
John Owen to Betsey Bristow, ___ 6, 1812.
John Waren, BM. (CA)
Gilbert Pool to Betsey Keys, Sep. 16, 1812.
Thomas Brown, BM. (Sep. 16, 1812) (CA)
Philip Pritchett to Peggy McDonald, July 2, 1812.
Jeremiah Shelly, BM. (CA)
Thomas Stephenson to Rhoda Crisp, July 21, 1812.
Tandy Lane, BM. (CA)
Everett Stubbs to Sally Ford, Sep. 29, 1812.
Jonathan Harvey, BM. (CA)
Abner Underwood to Polly Keys, Dec. 28, 1812.
(CA)
James Wilkinson to Lucy Rice, Sep. 5, 1812.
James Rice, BM. (HRC)

1813

Nathaniel Applegate to Elizabeth Seaton, Aug. 6, 1813.
George Cook, BM. (Aug. 6, 1813) (CA)
Joshua Birdwell to Mary Jeans, Aug. 18, 1813.
Moses Birdwell, BM. (CA)
Paul Blackburn to Patsey Reynolds, Sep. 1, 1813.
Talton Branham, BM. (CA)
William Bowman to Levisey Edwards (or Edmonds), Jan. 10,
1813. Mathew Edmond, BM. (CA)
Thomas Cannon to Elizabeth Manley, Aug. 26, 1813.
(CA)
Alexander Casey to Nancy Ross, Sep. 9, 1813.
William Brown, BM. (CA)
James Cooper to Mary Weir, Sep. 10, 1813.
Andrew Weir, BM. (HRC)
John Craig to Lucy Eaton, Jan. 7, 1813.
(CA)
James Lewis Crow to Pheba Rice, Jan. 10, 1813.
John Leftwick, BM. (CA)
John Derossett to Patsey Pritchett, Nov. 22, 1813.
(Nov. 22, 1813) (CA)
Joshua Dover to Passy Rice, Sep. 7 (or 11), 1813.
Abraham Stout, BM. (CA)
James Forrester to Polly Bryant, July 23,1813.
Samuel Stout, BM. (July 23, 1813) (CA)
Adam Gardenhire to Elesey Tippit, Dec. 24, 1813.
John Black, BM. (CA)

Nathan Gowen to Sebri Midgett, July 28, 1813.
David Brown, BM. (CA)
Peter Gray to Elizabeth Wester, June 16, 1813.
David Scrivner, BM. (CA)
Samuel Green to Martha Ferguson, _____, 1813(?).
(HRC)
Alfred Haggard to Lettice Mason, Feb. 20, 1813.
George Pickle, BM. (Feb. 20, 1813) (CA)
Samuel Hall to Jenny Lemmons, Apr. 2, 1813.
Axham Lawhorn, BM. (CA)
Hezikiah Hotchkiss to Lydia Mean, Jan. 5, 1813.
Benjamin Tippett, BM. (CA)
Edward Kenley to Polly Rusk, May 11, 1813.
(CA)
Charles Kitchen to Anna Matlock, Aug. 24, 1813.
John Allen, BM. (CA)
Aquilanes Lane to Sally Lee, Jan. 3, 1813.
William Gardenhire, BM. (CA)
John Moore to Catherine Waren, Aug. 2, 1813.
Edward Waren, BM. (CA)
William Moore to Unity Tucker, Oct. 28, 1813.
Wm. Davis, BM. (CA)
John Newman to Francis Brashears, Sep. 2, 1813.
Elisha Williamson, BM. (CA)
George Pickle to Susana Haggard, Feb. 1, 1813.
Daniel Grubb, BM. (CA)
Linsey Pololuson to Delilay Owens, Jan. 27, 1813.
Jason Roberts, BM. (CA)
Enoch Rector to Polly Kindrick, Aug. 31, 1813.
Richard Rector, BM. (Aug. 31, 1813) (CA)
William Reynolds to Jinny Moore, _____, 1813.
George Sirkle, BM. (CA)
Larkin Sawyer to Elizabeth Childs, Sep. 23, 1813.
William D. Neilson, BM. (HRC)
James Sisco to Sally Branham, June 29, 1813.
Thomas McMullin, BM. (CA)
Edward Stewart to Nancy Short, Dec. 2, 1813.
William Rorax, BM. (Dec. 2, 1813) (CA)
Augustus Strong to Louisa Shepherd, _____, 1813(?).
Townley Deakins, Thomas Oliver, BM. (CA)
Tandy Senter to Alice Crumbliss, Apr. 8, 1813.
James Crumbliss, BM. (CA)
William Thacker to Levina Eblin, Mar. 2, 1813.
(CA)
Jeremiah Tuton to Rebecca McNutt, June 18, 1813.
John McNutt, BM. (June 12 1813) (CA)
Wiley Tuton to Levina Bailey, Aug. 7, 1813.
William Brown, BM. (Aug. 17, 1813) (CA)
John Wilkerson to Anna Woods, Sep. 30, 1813.
(CA)
Edward Young to Sally Vaughn, May 29, 1813.
John Leftwick, BM. (CA)

1814

Nathaniel Applegate to Elizabeth Smith, Dec. 1, 1814.
Richard Faries, BM. (HRC)
Daniel Bailey to Nicey Vaughn, Feb. 10, 1814.
(HRC)
Smith Bonigan to Betsey Haley, Sep. 6, 1814.
John Carmichael, BM. (Sep. 6, 1814) (CA)
William Bower to Betsey Phillips, June (or July) 7, 1814.
John W. Bower, BM. (CA, HRC)
William Breeden to Patients Phippy, June 22, 1814.
James Hope, BM. (June 22, 1814) (CA)
James Flatt to Rebecca Rice, Oct. 17, 1814.
John Rice, BM. (Oct. 17, 1814) (CA)
Robert Harvey to Sally Richards, July 17, 1814.
Isham Young, BM. (CA)
Claiborn Kinman to Betsey Bower, Aug. 6, 1814.
James Bowers, BM. (Aug. 10, 1819) (CA)
Richard Lay to Jane Bryant, Mar. 10, 1814.
Mathew Gowen, BM. (CA)
John Lent to Molly M. Kain, Sep. 27, 1814.
Francis Green, BM. (CA)
David Lyles to Mary Tuton, June 23, 1814.
Joseph Hankins, BM. (CA)
Henry Matlock to Nancy Rice, Nov. 5, 1814.
John Purris, BM. (CA)
Charles Mitchell to Framinia Parriman, Feb. 16, 1814.
Lewis Combs, BM. (Feb. 16, 1814) (CA)
George Moore to Sally Rice, July 20, 1814.
Joseph Long, BM. (CA)
Samuel Owen to Nelly Randolph, Oct. 26, 1814.
Moses Russell, BM. (CA)
Benagah Pennington to Malinda Emery, July 26, 1814.
(CA)
Isaac Roberson (or Robinson) to Nancy Talbot, July 9
(or 30), 1814. Frances (or Francis) Erwin, BM. (CA,
HRC)
Moses Russell to Juda Owens, July 6, 1814.
Eli Shelton, BM. (CA)
Joseph Starkey to Rebecca Shadden, Nov. 20, 1814.
Robert Shadden, BM. (CA)
John Thomas to Barbara Casey, Dec. 1, 1814.
Anthony Casey, BM. (HRC)

1815

James Allsup to Pheby Childs, Jan. 12, 1815.
(CA)
Henry Anderson to Nancy Man, Aug. 28, 1815.
(CA)
Jonas Arnold to Ann Eblin, Dec. 31, 1815.
Willias Durrett, BM. (CA)
Fielding Bolden to Nancy Stean, Jan. 19, 1815.
Thomas York, BM. (Jan. 19, 1815) (CA, HRC)
Isaac Ciscow to Polly Draper, July 29, 1815.
(CA)

William Dixon to Lucy Harvey, Feb. 4, 1815.
Marmaduke Harvey, BM. (CA)
William Eblen to Lucretia Smith, Sep. 14, 1815.
(HRC)
Benjamin Eldridge to Patsey Jackson, Feb. 7, 1815.
John Harrison, BM. (CA)
Thomas Eldridge to Sally Warren, Dec. 14, 1815.
(CA)
John W. Estes to Polly Bristoe, May 11, 1815.
(CA)
Elijah Farmer to Jane Preston, May 2, 1815.
(HRC)
James Flatt to Rebecca Rice, Oct. 17, 1815.
John Rice, BM. (CA)
Elijah Foreman to Jane Preston, May 2, 1815.
(CA)
William Gillan to Betsie Bristoe, June 14, 1815.
Gilbreath Barton, BM. (CA)
James Gillispie to Jinny Gallaher, Feb. 10, 1815.
Thomas Gallaher, BM. (CA)
Samuel Grigsby to Polly Lindsey, Dec. 4, 1815.
Noah Ashley, BM. (Dec. 4, 1815) (CA)
Wright Hankins to Nancy Talent, Sep. 4, 1815.
(CA)
Hiram Hide to Rachel Irvin, Sep. 18, 1815.
(CA)
John Hill to Virry Lane, Jan. 6, 1815.
Joseph Graham, BM. (HRC)
Abraham Lacy to Betsey Allen, Oct. 26, 1815.
George Crow, BM. (CA)
Moses Mahan to Betsey Cleck (or Click), July 5, 1815.
(CA)
Jason Matlock, Jr. to Betsey Hicks, Sep. 30, 1815.
(CA, HRC)
Bartlet McAnelly to Phebe Shields, Mar. 16, 1815.
(CA)
John E. Nelson to Polly Daley, Jan. 30, 1815.
Asa Cobb, BM. (CA)
Littleberry Noe to Sally Sharp, Nov. 25, 1815.
(CA)
Joel Oliver to Celia Vaughn, Jan. 19 (or Aug. 8), 1815.
(CA, HRC)
Robert Rentfroe to Catherine Goodman, Nov. 13, 1815.
John Loyd, BM. (Nov. 13, 1815) (CA)
John B. Rice to Sally Brashear, Dec. 12, 1815.
(CA)
Gabriel Richards to Peggy Ayers, July 24, 1815.
(CA, HRC)
Robert Riley to Sally Field, Oct. 3, 1815.
(CA)
Audley Walker to Elizabeth McKamey, Oct. 10, 1815.
Samuel R. Walker, BM. (CA)
Edmond (or Edward) Warren to Polly Eldridge, Dec. 1, 1815.
(CA, HRC)

Benjamin Williams to Cizire, June 4, 1815.
Jacob Rector, BM. (CA)

1816

Abraham Adkinson (or Absolom Adkison) to Sally Adkinson
(or Adkison), Dec. 23, 1816. Benj. J. White, BM.
(Dec. 24, 1816) (CA)
David Adkison to Drusilla Foshee, Jan. 27, 1816.
Isaac McPherson (Jan. 29, 1816) (CA)
James Bower to Betsey Crow, Jan. 20, 1816.
William McKamy, BM. (Feb. 1, 1816) (CA)
John Bowman to Pegg Phillips, Apr. 22, 1816.
(Apr. 23, 1816) (CA)
Samuel Brashear to Hannah Tooten, Feb. 26, 1816.
(Feb. 29, 1816) (CA)
Walter Brashear to Elizabeth Roberts, Dec. 3, 1816.
Philip Roberts, BM. (Dec. 5, 1816) (CA)
Jacob Casner to Polly Matlock, Sep. 28, 1816.
(CA)
David Claunch to Betsey Pritchett, May 26, 1816.
Philip Pritchet, BM. (May 26, 1816) (CA)
David Craig to Jenney Eaton, Jan. 30, 1816.
James Dearmond, BM. (Jan. 31, 1816) (CA)
Harmon Culp to Jenny Eaton, July 22, 1816.
Jesse Pellain, BM. (July 23, 1816) (CA)
David Davenport to Lucinda Kinchelow, June 15, 1816.
Joseph Lacey, BM. (CA)
Abraham David to Rebecca Curtis, Sep. 19, 1816.
Shadrick Stephens, BM. (Oct. 3, 1816) (CA)
William Dudley to Sally Irwin, Sep. 6, 1816.
Jeremich Fields, BM. (CA)
Thomas Forrester to Peggy Marney, Dec. 24, 1816.
Uriah Allison, BM. (CA)
Wyatt, Gallaher to Sally Dalton, Oct. 12, 1816.
(Jan. 6, 1816) (CA)
Robert Gilliland to Peggy McNabb, June 13, 1816.
Wm. C. McKamy, BM. (June 13, 1816) (CA)
Able Gowers to Rachel Lay, Feb. 20, 1816.
James Lay, BM. (Feb. 21, 1816) (CA)
James Hamilton to Nancy Childres (or Childers), Nov. 22,
1816. Samuel Stout, BM. (Nov. 22, 1816) (CA)
Eli Hart to Nancy Littleton, Nov. 2, 1816.
Thomas Walker, BM. (Nov. 2, 1816) (CA)
John Hawkins to Priscilla McKinnie, Mar. 9, 1816.
Jesse Terry, BM. (____ 10, 1816) (CA)
Benjamin Haywood to Patsey Stephens, Aug. 1, 1816.
(CA)
John Hood to Elizabeth Sexton, July 4, 1816.
(CA)
Tarlton Hunt to Sally Glass, Nov. 12, 1816.
(CA)
William C. Kington to Rhoda Rector, Oct. 30, 1816.
Benjamin Rector, BM. (CA)

Charles Kirkpatrick to Harriet Churchill, Apr. 11, 1816.
(Apr. 11, 1816) (CA)
Charles Kitchelow (or Kinchelow) to Betsey Cannon,
Oct. 2, 1816. John Edwards, BM. (CA)
Thomas Kitchum to Nancy Warren, Mar. 20, 1816.
William C. McKamy, BM. (Mar. 21, 1816) (CA)
John M. Love to Peggy Moore, Mar. 20, 1816.
James Moore, BM. (Mar. 21, 1816) (CA)
Samuel Margrave to Grace Wroe, Aug. 7, 1816.
John Purris, BM. (Aug. 7, 1816) (CA)
William McCarty to Milly Loony, Dec. 30, 1816.
Isaac Baker, BM. (CA)
James McKamey to Polly Houston, Dec. 9, 1816.
(Dec. 10, 1816) (CA)
Joseph McMinn to Nancy Williams, Aug. 4, 1816.
John Williams, BM. (Aug. 4, 1816) (CA)
James Moore to Lucy Young, Feb. 22, 1816.
(Feb. 23, 1816) (CA)
Thomas Oden to Nancy Miller, Aug. 3, 1816.
(CA, HRC)
John Oliver to Elizabeth Gallaher, Mar. 11, 1816.
Robert Gallaher, BM. (Apr. 4, 1816) (CA)
Solomon Potter to Esther Melton, Dec. 13 (or 16), 1816.
_____ McConnell, BM. (Dec. 26, 1816) (CA, HRC)
Elijah Prewitt to Nancy Hannah, Mar. 13, 1816.
(CA)
George Reed to Deborah Cobb, Apr. 5, 1816.
(Apr. 9, 1816) (CA)
John Roberts to Elizabeth Blackwell, Mar. 2, 1816.
Edward Robert, BM. (Mar. 3, 1816) (CA)
Lewis Robinson to Betsey Starks, Jan. 28, 1816.
(CA, HRC)
Mishac Rowden to Sarah McNabb, May 3, 1816.
(CA, HRC)
Phillip Rushing to Sally Breding, Sep. 8, 1816.
Mark Rentfro, BM. (CA)
John Scott to Nelly McDaniel, Nov. 12, 1816.
George Morefield, BM. (Nov. 16, 1816) (CA)
Anthony Smith to Ann Bailey, Sep. 3, 1816.
Robert S. Gilliland, BM. (CA)
Charles Stephens to Sally Margrave, Sep. 26, 1816.
George Grigsby, BM. (Sep. 26, 1816) (CA)
John Stow to Permealy Lane, Aug. 12, 1816.
Samuel Stow, BM. (Aug. 11, 1816) (CA)
Samuel Stow to Betsey Littleton, Nov. 21, 1816.
James Littleton, BM (CA)
Holston Todd to Peggy McPherson, Jan. 27, 1816.
William Brown, BM. (Feb. 1, 1816) (CA)
John Tucker to Jinny Moore, Jul. 9, 1816.
(CA)
William Vaughn to Milly Preston, Sep. 26, 1816.
(CA)
William Wallace to Sarah Wallace, Feb. 20, 1816.
Robert Thompson, BM. (Feb. 20, 1816) (CA)

Nicholas West to Polly Jackson, Dec. 17, 1816.
    John West, BM. (Dec. 19, 1816) (CA, HRC)
Calvin White to Patsey Wiley, July 29, 1816.
    William Galbreath, BM. (Aug. 1, 1816) (CA)
Uriah Wilkerson to Nancy Wood, Oct. 12, 1816.
    Willis Stockton, BM. (Oct. 12, 1816) (CA)
Thomas York to Elizabeth McPherson, July 27, 1816.
    (CA)

1817

Gabriel Adkins to Eleanor Mead, Aug. 21, 1817.
    John Mean, BM. (HRC)
Noah Ashley to Bertha Good, Apr. 20, 1817.
    Edward Good, BM. (Apr. 20, 1817)
William Bailey to Betsey Lawson, Dec. 17, 1817.
    Bertley Lawson, BM. (Dec. 18, 1817) (CA)
Richard Branham to Rebecca Witt, July 8, 1817.
    Tarlton Branham, BM. (CA)
Benjamin Franklin Breazeale to Patsey Miller, Mar. 26,
    1817. Henry Breazeale, Tho. Breazeale, BM. (CA)
John Breeden to Nancy Frost, Sep. 10, 1817.
    William McKamey, BM. (HRC)
Beveredge (or Bevinds) Brown to Jenny Mathews, Feb. 27,
    1817. Nicholas Mansfield, BM. (Feb. 27, 1817) (CA, HRC)
Joseph Byrd to Phemy Mulky, Feb. 21, 1817.
    Samuel Stout, BM. (Feb. 2, 1817) (CA)
Robert Campbell to Sally Lacky, Sep. 2, 1817.
    James Lacky, BM. (Sep. 4, 1817) (CA)
George Carter to Peggy Dunningan, Nov. 22, 1817.
    John Brown, BM. (Nov. 27, 1817) (CA)
Alexander Casey to Eany Whith, Nov. 24, 1817.
    Samuel Tucker, BM. (HRC)
Jesse Casey to Patsey Coe, Apr. 4, 1817.
    John Thomas, BM. (May 10, 1817) (CA, HRC)
Isaac Casner to Mary Cook, Dec. 3, 1817.
    John Loyd, BM. (CA)
Caleb Casteel to Susana Whittenburger, Jan. 2, 1817.
    Samuel Wilson, BM. (Jan. 2, 1817) (CA)
Seaborn Center to Nancy Carson, Aug. 28, 1817.
    George Arnold, BM. (Aug. 28, 1817) (CA, HRC)
William Click to Phebe Longacre, Nov. 29, 1817.
    Joseph Longacre, BM. (CA)
Arthur Coody (or Cody) to Synthea Garrett, Apr. 5, 1817.
    Thomas Clark, BM. (CA, HRC)
Thomas Cox to Nancy Vaughn, May 11, 1817.
    Isiah Brown, BM. (May 11, 1817) (CA, HRC)
Edward Crow to Jinny Burns, Jan. 29, 1817.
    (Jan. 30, 1817) (CA)
Bradley Dalton to Sally Silvey, Jan. 22, 1817.
    William Silvey, BM. (CA)
Nathan Daniel to Celia Lammons, June 21, 1817.
    Isaac England, BM. (CA)
Asa Davis to Ann Wilkerson, June 5, 1817.
    Wm. C. McKamy, BM. (July 20, 1817) (CA)

Jonathan Dildine to Nancy Garrett, Dec. 30, 1817.
   Gillesreath Barton, BM. (HRC)
Charles Dowers to Anna Shields, July 21, 1817.
   (July 26, 1817) (CA)
Samuel Eblen to Sally McCown, June 21, 1817.
   (June 26, 1817) (CA)
Jacob Elkins to Ann Gowers, Dec. 30, 1817.
   Samuel Davis, BM. (Dec. 30, 1817) (CA)
Isaac England to Rebecca Rector, Oct. 11, 1817.
   Thomas England, BM. (Oct. 11, 1817) (CA, HRC)
Lewis Fairchilds to Malony Melton, Apr. 25, 1817.
   Abraham Justice, BM. (CA)
Alexander Forrester to Sally Harvey, Dec. 11, 1817.
   John McClellan, BM. (Dec. 11, 1817) (CA)
Nathan Gann to Sarah Delaney, Dec. 24, 1817.
   (Dec. 24, 1817) (CA)
William Gilbreath to Synthia Garrett, Aug. 10, 1817.
   James G. Williams, BM. (CA)
James Glasgow, Jr. to Lyda White, Feb. 6, 1817.
   William Brown, BM. (Feb. 6, 1817) (CA)
Jesse Goddard to Polly Center, Nov. 17, 1817.
   James Center, BM. (CA)
John Green to Polly Price, Dec. 20, 1817.
   (Dec. 25, 1817) (CA)
Joseph Hankins to Isabella Miller, Oct. 24, 1817.
   (CA)
Joseph Hankins to Keziah Reynolds, Mar. 27, 1817.
   John Purris, BM. (Apr. 10, 1817) (CA)
William Harwick to Zilphia McNutt, Jan. 8, 1817.
   Wm. McClellan, BM. (Jan. 16, 1817) (CA)
Morgan Hendrix to Sally Bowman, May 21, 1817.
   Garrett Hall, BM. (CA)
Welcom Howell to Ann Longaire, Aug. 19, 1817.
   Asa Howell, BM. (CA)
Peter Johnson to Keziah Berry (or Barry), Feb. 16, 1817.
   John Leftwick, BM. (Feb. 16, 1817) (CA, HRC)
Waitman Jones to Hessy Stewart, Mar. 6, 1817.
   William Stewart, BM. (CA)
Alexander Kelly to Sally Prigmore, Feb. 17, 1817.
   George Gregsby, BM. (HRC)
William Kernealson to Peggy Headrick, Feb. 10, 1817.
   Peter Tidwell, BM. (CA)
Joseph Knox to Margaret Erwin, Sep. 5 (or 6), 1817.
   John Rather, BM. (Sep. 11, 1817) (CA, HRC)
Jacob Lemmons to Louisa Winters, Apr. 12, 1817.
   Thos. C. Childress, BM. (May 1, 1817) (CA)
Moses Looney to Polly (or Patty) York, Feb. 27, 1817.
   Joseph Lacy, BM. (Mar. 2, 1817) (CA)
Hugh McFail to Isabella McKamy, Sep. 1, 1817.
   Joseph McPherson, BM. (Sep. 2, 1817) (CA)
Wm. McNutt to Sally Dixon, Dec. 30, 1817.
   David Scrivner, BM. (Dec. 20, 1817) (CA)
James Moore to Nancy Lanston, Nov. 26, 1817.
   Benjamin Hagewood, Philip Stephens, BM. (Nov. 26, 1817)
   (CA, HRC)

Andrew Nail to Sally Harris (or Harvey), Apr. (or
  Sep.) 20, 1817. Allen Hill, BM. (CA, HRC)
Joseph Nail to Albina Minsco White, Mar. 4 (or 14), 1817.
  (Mar. 6, 1817) (CA, HRC)
Conrad Newman to Cazea Reynolds, Dec. 18, 1817.
  Elisha William, BM. (CA)
Eli Oliver to Espere Ellis, Mar. 10, 1817.
  Thomas C. Childres, BM. (CA)
John H. Price to Harriet Williams, July 21, 1817.
  (Aug. 1, 1817) (CA)
John Punnell to Nancy McAnally, Sep. 11, 1817.
  John Leftwick, BM. (CA)
John Rather to Nancy Nail, May 8, 1817.
  William Gardenhire, BM. (HRC)
William Roach to Sarah Spears, Sep. 16, 1817.
  Joseph Holloway, BM. (CA)
Stephen Shadrick to Susanna Willaism, Oct. 7, 1817.
  (Oct. 9, 1817) (CA)
William Silvey to Patsey Silvey, Dec. 8, 1817.
  (Dec. 10, 1817) (CA)
Phillip Stephens to Mary Oliver, Dec. 5, 1817.
  George Stephens, BM. (HRC)
William Taylor to Rachel Crow, Nov. 10, 1817.
  James G. Williams, BM. (HRC)
Andrew Thomas to Polly Larramore, Nov. 11, 1817.
  (CA)
Peter Upshaw to Jenny Fields, Jan. 14 (or 16), 1817.
  Bradley Dalton, BM. (Jan. 15, 1817) (CA, HRC)
James Wells to Majory Moore, Oct. 11, 1817.
  Hugh Woody, BM. (CA)
John West to Sally Chamblee, May 31, 1817.
  (CA)
Samuel Woods to Hannah Woody, Mar. 25, 1817.
  (CA, HRC)

1818

William Bailey to Franky Rayborn, Aug. 18 (or 19), 1818.
  Daniel Bailey, BM. (Aug. 20, 1818) (CA, HRC)
John Barger to Polly Lacky, Mar. 10, 1818.
  James Lacky, BM. (Mar. 18, 1818) (CA)
Thomas Branham to Nelly Branham (of Knox County),
  Dec. 29, 1818. Nicholas Mansfield, BM. (Dec. 30, 1818)
  (CA, HRC)
Alexander Brown to Polly Sharp, Mar. 19, 1818.
  Thomas Brown, BM. (Mar. 19, 1818) (CA, HRC)
Zachariah Casteel to Rebecca Hartley, _____, 1818(?).
  Married in Green County, moved to Roane County in
  1821. (HRC)
James Cox to Barbara Gardener, Sep. 11, 1818.
  James Gardner, BM. (Sep. 13, 1818) (CA, HRC)
George Dennis to Barbara Harris, Aug. 25, 1818.
  David Shakeford, BM. (CA)
Osy Dixon to Jinny Boden, Dec. 29, 1818.
  Benjamin Porter, BM. (CA, HRC)

John Douty to Betsey Holland, Dec. 22, 1818.
    Sam'l Silvey, BM. (Dec. 29, 1818) (CA)
John Durrett to Sarah Hamelton, Jan. 19, 1818.
    John Purris, BM. (Jan. 22, 1818) (CA)
Martin Durret to Rebecah White, Mar. 28, 1818.
    Rudolph Moreman, BM. See also Martin Durrett, 1822.
    (CA)
William Erwin to Drusilla Hannah, Mar. 13, 1818.
    Joseph Duncan, BM. (CA, HRC)
Jacob Fritts to Sally Sexton, Dec. 23, 1818.
    John Fritts, BM. (HRC)
Isaac Funk to Rebecca Rayburn, Sep. 18, 1818.
    Jesse Rayburn, BM. (Oct 1, 1818) (CA)
William Hampton to Peggy Burk, Dec. 23, 1818.
    John Fritts, BM. (Dec. 30, 1818) (CA)
Henry Hart to Polly Snow, Feb. 3, 1818.
    James G. Williams, BM. (HRC)
Vinet Henry to Roaanna(?) Lower, Dec. 21, 1818.
    Jonas Arnold, BM. (Dec. 22, 1818) (CA)
James Hornsby to Elinor McKidy, Jan. 5, 1818.
    (CA)
Charles Isham to Mary Barnett, Mar. 8, 1818.
    Henry Isham, BM. (CA)
Oxley Johnson to Catey Rogers, Oct. 16, 1818.
    Richard Dickens, BM. (Oct. 16, 1818) (CA, HRC)
William King to Fanny Gains, June 19, 1818.
    Uriah Allison, BM. (June 20, 1818) (CA)
John Leadsinger to Joanna Bucklen, May 6, 1818.
    Ruben Williams, BM. (CA)
Luke Lyttle to Mary Casteel, Jan. 7, 1818.
    Edmond Casteel, BM. (CA, HRC)
James McCampbell to Betsey Clark, Apr. 2, 1818.
    William Alexander, BM. (Apr. 2, 1818) (CA)
Joseph McClenchan (or McClellan) to Jinny Moore,
    Mar. 17, 1818. John Kenely, BM. (CA, HRC)
Samuel McClellan to Ann Twitty, Mar. 14, 1818.
    Abraham McClellan, BM. (Mar. 17, 1818) (CA)
David McDaniel to Mary Buchanan, Mar. 4 (or 14), 1818.
    Peter Manning, BM. (Mar. 15, 1818) (CA, HRC)
John McRoberts to Mary Hale, Jan. 17, 1818.
    Barton McPherson, BM. (CA)
Richard Melton to Polly Green, Jan. 6, 1818.
    (Jan. 8, 1818) (CA)
Edward Merritt to Sally Carden, June 27, 1818.
    Sam'l Grigsby (or Gisley), BM. (July 2, 1818) (CA, HRC)
Rudolph Moorman to Rebecca White, Mar. 28, 1818.
    Martin Durrett, BM. (HRC)
Edward Musgrove to Nancy Stout, June 12, 1818.
    Rudolph Meraman, BM. (June 14, 1818) (CA, HRC)
Jesse Power to Betsey Baker, Aug. 19, 1818.
    John Brown, BM. (CA)
Jesse Raben to Susanna Funk, Mar. 24, 1818.
    Samuel Marney, BM. (Mar. 27, 1818) (CA)
Thomas Scott to Sarah Ferguson, Oct. 6, 1818.
    Pleasant Branham, BM. (Oct. 6, 1818) (CA)

George Reynolds to Rachel Smith, Sep. 24, 1818.
James Moore, James Renolds, BM. (Sep. 24, 1818)
(CA, HRC)
David Shaw to Chryleena Vickey, Nov. 23, 1818.
James Lackey, BM. (HRC)
John Shirley (or Shields) to Nellie Delozier, Mar. 23,
1818. James Kennon, BM. (CA, HRC)
Willia Short to Nancy Kindrick, Nov. 20, 1818.
Edward Stewart, BM. (CA)
William Silvey to Betsey Howard, Oct. 5, 1818.
Samuel Silvey, BM. (Oct. 8, 1818) (CA)
Robert Spence to Margaret Alexander, Feb. 14, 1818.
James Lackey, BM. (CA)
Abner Staples to Elery Toomey, May 6, 1818.
Ambrose Toomey, BM. (HRC)
John M. Staples to Polly Bryant, Dec. 7, 1818.
Sam'l S. Walker, BM. (Dec. 10, 1818) (CA)
William Uteley to Fanny Blake, Nov. 3, 1818.
Pleasant Brannum, BM. (Nov. 3, 1818) (CA)
Samuel Watson to Francis Browder, Apr. 2, 1818.
George Selvage, BM. (Apr. 9, 1818) (CA)
Luther White to Isabella McKamy, Jan. 27, 1818.
William White, BM. (Feb. 5, 1818) (CA, HRC)
Elisha Williamson to Rebecca Mann, Oct. 20 (or 26), 1818.
(CA, HRC)
Jesse Wood to Elizabeth Siscoe, Dec. 9, 1818.
James Preston, BM. (Dec. 13, 1818) (CA)

1819

John Acard to Sarah Turner, July 28, 1819.
(CA)
William Arnold to Martha D. King, Aug. 17, 1819.
J. R. T. King, BM. (Aug. 17, 1819) (CA, HRC)
Elijah Baker to Jane Sexton, Nov. 31, 1819.
Thomas Childress, BM. (CA)
Arthur Bane to Elener McPherson, May 4, 1819.
William Jent, BM. (HRC)
James Beaverz to Betsey Foshee, May 27, 1819.
Azariah Cooper, BM. (First Thurs. of June) (CA)
Abner Blanton to Nancy Stultz (or Shultz), Aug. 4, 1819.
Lansford Fields, BM. (Aug. 7, 1819) (CA, HRC)
John Bowers to Polly Crow, Dec. 6, 1819.
James Bowers, BM. (HRC)
James Brown to Betsey Hacker, Feb. 6, 1819.
Allen Sneed, BM. (Feb. 7, 1819) (CA)
John Brown to Polly Crow, Dec. 6, 1819.
James Brown, BM. (Dec. 22, 1819) (CA)
Green M. Bruce to Nancy McCabe, Oct. 9, 1819.
Robert S. Gilliland, BM. (HRC)
Joseph Bryant to Patsey Hart, Feb. 10, 1819.
John Loyd, BM. (Feb. 11, 1819) (CA, HRC)
Robert Bush to Nellie Williamson, Dec. 7, 1819.
Wm. C. McKamy, BM. (Dec. 9, 1819) (CA)

ROANE COUNTY MARRIAGES

Joseph Byrd to Ann Pride, May 6, 1819.
  Thomas Brown, BM. (CA, HRC)
Charles Clark to Mary Rector, Oct. 4, 1819.
  John W. Clark, BM. (CA)
James Coody to Polly Cart, Dec. 29, 1819.
  Philip Pritchett, BM. (CA)
Solomon Copeland to Sarah Tippett, July 12, 1819.
  James Tippett, BM. (CA)
Thomas Coppage to Betsey Allison, Mar. 27, 1819.
  John McEwen, BM. (HRC)
John Coulson to Sallie Ketching, Mar. 17, 1819.
  William Long, BM. (HRC)
William Crow to Patsey Bower, Dec. 16, 1819.
  James Bower, BM. (Dec. 21, 1819) (CA, HRC)
Willis Crow to Nancy Tedder, Dec. 1, 1819.
  (Jan. 2, 1820) (CA, HRC)
Richard Curd (or Card) to Polly Eldridge, Nov. 29, 1819.
  Benjamin Eldridge, BM. (Dec. 2, 1819) (CA, HRC)
Lewis DeRossett to Isbel Lane, Sep. 1, 1819.
  John J. Breazeale, BM. (CA, HRC)
Joseph Duncan to Rebeckah Irwin, Jan. 28, 1819.
  Edward McKane, BM. (Jan. 28, 1819) (CA)
Willis Durrett to Polly Copher, Feb. 3, 1819.
  Benjamin C. White, BM. (Feb. 4, 1819) (CA)
John Eblen to Nancy McMullin, Mar. 22, 1819.
  (Mar. 25, 1819) (CA)
John A. Foshee to Malinda Cooper, Oct. 26, 1819.
  Josiah Fike, BM. (Oct. 29, 1819) (CA)
Thomas Gossage to Betsey Allison, Mar. 22, 1819.
  John McEwin, BM. (Mar. 25, 1819) (CA)
Bruce Green to Nancy McCabe, Oct. 19, 1819.
  Robt S. Gilliland, BM. (CA)
William Green to Mary Smith, Mar. 15, 1819.
  Anthony Dickey, BM. (HRC)
John Hankins to Betsey Oliver, Dec. 30, 1819.
  (CA)
Samuel Harris to Peggy McVay (or McVey), Nov. 8, 1819.
  Wyatt Gallaher, BM. (Nov. 9, 1819) (CA, HRC)
William Hawkins to Kitty Funk, Mar. 25, 1819.
  Jesse Preston, BM. (Mar. 30, 1819) (CA)
Benjamin Hayewood to Polly Robinson, Apr. 10, 1819.
  Edward Warren, BM. (Apr. 11, 1819) (CA, HRC)
William Headrick to Matilda Short, Mar. 12, 1819.
  William Cornealison, BM. (HRC)
Albert Henderson to Elizabeth Hawks, Aug. 16, 1819.
  Wm. H. Lay, BM. (CA)
Micajah Howerton to Jane Brown, Aug. 19, 1819.
  (Aug. 19, 1819) (CA)
James Humphreys to Polly West, Oct. 10, 1819.
  George Branham, BM. (Oct. 18, 1819) (CA, HRC)
Isiah Jackson to Polly Browder, Nov. 23, 1819.
  (Nov. 25, 1819) (CA)
Alexander Kelly to Sally Prigmore, Feb. 17, 1819.
  George Grigsby, BM. (Feb. 17, 1819) (CA)

Claborn Kinnan to Betsy Bowers, Aug. 6, 1819.
(HRC)
James Laramore (or Lanman) of Knox Co., Tenn., to
Katy (or Kitty) Thomas, Jan. 11, 1819. James Nipper,
BM. (Jan 11, 1819) (CA, HRC)
James Littleton to Kitty Brown, Dec. 30, 1819.
(Dec. 30, 1819) (CA)
Nicholas Mansfield to Jenny Morris, Feb. 20, 1819.
(Feb. 21, 1819) (CA, HRC)
Samuel Marney to Elizabeth Spence, May 1, 1819.
Richard Richards, BM. (May 2, 1819) (CA, HRC)
Daniel Mason to Patsey Hicks, May 20, 1819.
John Purris, BM. (CA)
William Mason to Sophia Work, Aug. 4, 1819.
Wm. C. McChany (or McKamey), BM. (CA, HRC)
William McConnell to Jane Scott, Jan. 23 (or 28), 1819.
John Potter, BM. (Feb. 4, 1819) (CA, HRC)
Alexander McCullock to Lucy Robinson, Mar. 1, 1819.
Levi Wheat, BM. (HRC)
Caleb McDonald (or McDaniel) to Susanna Carter,
Nov. 19 (or 23), 1819. David McDonald (or David
McDaniel), BM. (CA, HRC)
Samuel McMullin to Jane Baily, Nov. 13, 1819.
Noah Ashley, BM. (Nov. 17, 1819) (CA, HRC)
John McNutt to Lucresa Rayburn, Mar. 25, 1819.
Thomas Rayburn, BM. (Mar. 26, 1819) (CA, HRC)
Nathan Padget to Kiziah Allen, Feb. 8, 1819.
Uriah Allison, BM. (Feb. 8, 1821) (CA)
Abner Parks, to Viney Lane, Feb. 25, 1819.
Thomas Prigmore, BM. (CA, HRC)
Matthis Parr to Sally Kimbrel, Feb. 20, 1819.
David Parr, BM. (CA)
Samuel Prater to Isabella Blair, Sep. 8, 1819.
James Blair, BM. (CA)
Hezekiah Quick to _____, Mar. 20, 1819.
Isham Cox, Sr., BM. (HRC)
John Rice to Tabitha Dodson, Aug. 18, 1819.
William Matlock, BM. (HRC)
Loony Riley to Rachel Stewart, Aug. 28, 1819.
Isaac Keys, BM. (Aug. 29, 1819) (CA)
Samuel Selbe to Sally Cook, Nov. 4, 1819.
William Selbe, BM. (Nov. 4, 1819) (CA)
Charles Shoemaker to Betsey Toneary, Sep. 7, 1819.
Charles White, BM. (CA)
William Steane (or Sloane) to Elizabeth Rector, Sep. 13,
1819. John Jackson, BM. (CA, HRC)
Samuel Swan to Nancy McElwee, Dec. 21, 1819.
(Dec. 21, 1819) (CA)
John Taylor to Nancy Crow, Sep. 6, 1819.
(Sep. 6, 1819) (CA)
Thomas Taylor to Mary Ann McAnally, Feb. 24, 1819.
David Webster, BM. (CA)
John Tedder to Mary Robinson, Feb. 4, 1819.
Uriah Allison, BM. (Feb. 4, 1819) (CA, HRC)

Baldwin Underwood to Margaret White, Apr. 17, 1819.
  Lemson Copher, BM. (CA)
John Vincent to Anna Mosse, Feb. 16, 1819.
  John Thomas, BM. (HRC)
Jesse Waten to Mary Moore, Nov. 13, 1819.
  William Leftwich, BM. (HRC)
Ruben Williams to Mahulda Cobb, Nov. 24, 1819.
  Rudolph Moorman, BM. (Dec. 7, 1819) (CA)
John M. Wilson to Anna D. Rogers, Feb. 22, 1819.
  Thomas Rogers, BM. (Feb. 25, 1819) (CA)

1820

Uriah Allison to Nancy (or Mary) Cox, Jan. 20 (or 29),
  1820. Thomas Brown, BM. (Feb. 1, 1820) (CA, HRC)
Isaac Anderson to Julian Fout, Oct. 13, 1820.
  William Berry, BM. (HRC)
Stephen Anderson to Eliza Pritchett, Feb. 26, 1820.
  (CA)
John Barnett to Cinthea Small, July 26, 1820.
  Anthony Hewitt, BM. (July 27, 1820) (CA)
Wm. Beavers to Betsey Cravet, July 24, 1820.
  James Beavers, BM. (Aug. 10, 1820) (CA, HRC)
Philip Beddo to Kitty Parr, Feb. 8, 1820.
  (CA)
Frencis (or Francis) Benton to Nancy Cooly, Mar. 22, 1820.
  Sawyer Hart, BM. (CA)
William Bogart to Polly Preston, Sep. 7, 1820.
  Abraham Bogart, BM. (CA, HRC)
Isiah R. Brown to Margaret Sharp, Sep. 26, 1820.
  James Buchanan, BM. (Sep. 26, 1820) (CA)
Samuel Burnett to Sally Davis, Jan. 8, 1820.
  Thomas Spence, BM. (CA, HRC)
Elias Butler to Elizabeth Winters, Feb. 24, 1820.
  John Rector, BM. (Feb. 29, 1820) (CA)
Jesse Carter to Betsey Sutton, _____, 1820.
  James Sutton, BM. (CA)
William Caves (or Cavy) to Jinny Ireland, Nov. 20, 1820.
  Barney Casteel, BM. (CA)
John Clark to Jinny McPherson, Mar. 22 (or 27), 1820.
  Rudolph Moorman, BM (CA, HRC)
James Crumbliss to Ann Goddard, Nov. 15, 1820.
  Jesse Goddard, BM. (Nov. 16, 1820) (CA)
William DeRossett to Mary Ann Elkins, Oct. 10, 1820.
  Uriah Allison, BM. (Oct. 10, 1820) (CA)
Ruben Draper to Lucinda Williams, Jan. 5, 1820.
  (CA)
William Duel to Sarah Duncan, Apr. 11, 1820.
  Elijah Baker, BM. (Apr. 11, 1820) (CA)
Evan Duncan to Elizabeth Jinkins, Dec. 7, 1820.
  William Smith, BM. (CA)
Thos. Edminston to Nancy Box, Aug. 22, 1820.
  John Edminston, BM. (CA, HRC)
Michael Ethridge (or Etheridge) to Charity Hones (or
  Horne), Nov. 20 (or 24), 1820. Robert Marney, BM.
  (CA, HRC)

Solomon Forrester to Sarah Marney, June 22, 1820.
John Loyd, BM. (June 22, 1820) (CA, HRC)
James H. Gallaher to Isabella McClure, Nov. 4, 1820.
(Nov. 7, 1820) (CA)
Levi Galloway to Betsey Rector, June 17, 1820.
Jesse Galloway, BM. (June 27, 1820) (CA)
Mathew Gardenhire to Nancy Silvy, Feb. 3, 1820.
(CA)
William Green to Ruth Westmoreland, Mar. 29, 1820.
Benjamin Breshears, BM. (Mar. 30, 1820) (CA, HRC)
A. E. Griffith to Delia Potter, Mar. 21, 1820.
Absolom Potter, BM. (CA)
Archibald Harris to Charlotte Bendy, Oct. 14, 1820.
(CA)
James Hawkins (or Hankins) to Rebecca Fulton, Jan. 27,
1820. Robert Stone (or Stout), BM. (Feb. 3, 1820)
(CA, HRC)
George Henry to Lucy Lower, Feb. 16, 1820.
Jonas Arnold, BM. (CA)
Phillip Horner to Sarah Clark, Oct. 27, 1820.
Uriah Allison, BM. (CA, HRC)
Benjamine Howard to Mahaly M. Conk, Nov. 24, 1820.
Samuel Side, BM. (HRC)
Byrd Irwin to Elizabeth Burnett, Sep. 20, 1820.
John Breazeale, BM. (CA)
Henry Kindrick to Nancy Smith, May 16, 1820.
Rudolph Moorman, BM. (CA)
Nelson Ladd to Jenny Rogers, Dec. 23, 1820.
John C. Ladd, BM. (Dec. 28, 1820) (CA, HRC)
John Loller(?) to Patsey Daniel, Sep. 23, 1820.
(Sep. 24, 1820) (CA)
William Longacre to Patsey Colier, Nov. 28, 1820.
William Howel, BM. (Nov. 30, 1820) (CA)
Hezekiah Love to Martha Terry, Sep. 9, 1820.
Jessy Terry, BM. (Sep. 10, 1820) (CA)
Robert Martin to Patsey Nance, Dec. 23, 1820.
Joseph Ashley, BM. (Dec. 24, 1820) (CA, HRC)
George Martin to Elizabeth McIntire, Sep. 24, 1820.
John Martin, BM. (CA)
Clayton McCormick to Betsey Evans, Mar. 9, 1820.
Wiley Tuton, BM. (CA)
Absolom (or Abraham) Miller to Patsey West, Dec. 23, 1820.
James H. Miller, BM. (Dec. 28, 1820) (CA, HRC)
Dobson Miller to Maryana Burnett, July 17, 1820.
John Breazeale, BM. (Aug. 8, 1820) (CA)
James Moore to Jinny Woody, Jan. 10, 1820.
James McMullin, BM. (Jan. 10, 1820) (CA, HRC)
John Moore to Charity McDaniel, Nov. 1, 1820.
(HRC)
John Moses to Betsy Price (or Pelfrey), Sep. 5, 1820.
Nathan Turner, BM. (CA, HRC)
Andrew Nail to Nancy Stubbs, Jan. 15, 1820.
William Nail, BM. (Jan. 20, 1820) (CA, HRC)
Alfred Owens to Polly Long, Feb. 22, 1820.
Milton (or Martin) Center, BM. (CA, HRC)

John Pepper to Jenny Snow, Aug. 7, 1820.
Solomon Stow, BM. (Aug. 20, 1820) (CA)
David Phillips to Nancy Fike, Mar. 6, 1820.
Azarah Cooper, BM. (Mar. 7, 1820) (CA)
Jesse Preston to Nancy Bogart, Mar. 18 (or 27), 1820.
Abraham Bogart, BM. (CA, HRC)
Samuel Ramsey to Nancy Garner (or Gardner), Feb. 26, 1820.
Michael Sellers, BM. (Mar. 2, 1820) (CA, HRC)
Tyre Rogers to Polly Hart, June 9, 1820.
Wm. McKamy, BM. (June 9, 1820) (CA)
Jeremiah Salvage to Lucinda Cooly, July 12, 1820.
Thomas Stout, BM. (July 13, 1820) (CA)
John Selbe to Rhoday Cunningham, Sep. 5 (or 9), 1820.
George Arnold, Edward Warren, BM. (CA, HRC)
William Smith to Elly Collier, Dec. 1, 1820.
Washington Henderson, BM. (Dec. 10, 1820) (CA)
Samuel Stivers to Lucy Haley, Dec. 19, 1820.
Thos. Brown, BM. (CA)
James Stults to Fanny Davis, Dec. 9, 1820.
Brittain Davis, BM. (Dec. 12, 1820) (CA)
John Thompson to Nancy Rector, Nov. 28, 1820.
Landon Rector, BM. (Nov. 30, 1820) (CA)
Samuel Walker to Elizabeth Crisp, Aug. 2, 1820.
James Crisp, BM. (Aug. 6, 1820) (CA)
Jesse West to Susanna Carroll, July 31, 1820.
John Harrison, BM. (Aug. 3, 1820) (CA)
Benjamin Whittenburger to Lucinda Burnett, Mar. 27, 1820.
(Mar. 30, 1820) (CA)

1821

James Adkinson to Patsey McCabe, Feb. 7, 1821.
G. W. Bruce, BM. (CA)
Robert Allison to Nancy Byrd, Apr. 4, 1821.
Uriah Allison, BM. (Apr. 5, 1821) (CA, HRC)
Isaac Anderson to Julia Fout, Oct. 13, 1821.
Wm. W. Berry, BM. (Oct. 17, 1821) (CA)
Mathew Anderson to Polly Ellis, Nov. 22, 1821.
(Nov. 25, 1821) (CA)
James Baker to Betsey Weese, Nov. 12, 1821.
John Weese, BM. (Nov. 12, 1821) (CA)
Samuel Barnard to Nancy Jolly, July 10, 1821.
(July 12, 1821) (CA)
Armstead Blackwell to Betsey Galloway, Apr. 4, 1821.
Jesse Galloway, BM. (May 6, 1821) (CA, HRC)
Thomas Blake to Lucinda Hunter, June 6, 1821.
Etheldred Taylor, BM. (CA)
William Bowman to Betsey Hostler, Jan. 10, 1821.
Daniel Wester, BM. (Jan. 11, 1821) (CA)
Henry Breazeale to Patsey (or Betsey) Morgan, Mar. 2 (or
21), 1821. David Breazeale, BM. (Mar. 22, 1821) (CA, HRC)
John Breazeale to Anna Essary, Jan. 29, 1821.
John Essary, BM. (Feb. 1, 1821) (CA, HRC)
Robert Breazeale to Anna McKamey, Apr. 11, 1821.
Wm. Breazeale, BM. (CA)

ROANE COUNTY MARRIAGES

Rowland Chiles to Nancy Galloway, Apr. 5, 1821.
Jesse Galloway, BM. (Apr! 5, 1821) (CA, HRC)
Solomon Collins to Catey Arsterton, Mar. 21, 1821.
Moses Stout, BM. (HRC)
Alexander Cox to Sarah West, Feb. 8, 1821.
Lewis Burris, BM. (CA)
Thomas Dalton to Abby Evans, Dec. 26, 1821.
William Galbreath, BM. (CA)
Thomas Earle to Sally Blackwell, Feb. 21, 1821.
Archibald Earle, BM. (CA)
Samuel Erwin to Sally Ingram, Jan. 24, 1821.
Joseph Hankins, BM. (HRC)
Josiah Fike to Amy Sutton, July 7, 1821.
(July 10, 1821) (CA)
James Freeman to Axey Ponder, Oct. 17, 1821.
(HRC)
John Funk to Elizabeth Reed, Sep. 12, 1821.
(Sep. 12, 1821) (CA)
Robert Gamble to Betsy Lamb, May 12, 1821.
Gideon Morgan, BM. (HRC)
William Gay to Betsey Stults, May 3, 1821.
John Stults, BM. (May 6, 1821) (CA)
Theodorick Green to Mary Hostler, Dec. 15, 1821.
(Dec. 20, 1821) (CA)
Robert Grevat to Susanna West, Aug. 15, 1821.
(Aug. 19, 1821) (CA)
William Hall to Sarah Buchanan, Aug. 28, 1821.
(Aug. 29, 1821) (CA, HRC)
John Hendreck to Mariah Work, Apr. 14, 1821.
Samuel Woody, BM. (CA)
Joseph Henry to Scyntha Herbert, Jan. 24, 1821.
Michael Arnold, BM. (Feb. 1, 1821(?)) (CA, HRC)
Robert Hooper to Polly Goddard, Mar. 31, 1821.
John Brown, BM. (CA)
William Hornsby to Rachel Longacre, Apr. 14, 1821.
John Montgomery, BM. (CA)
Adam Houston to Zelpe Good, Apr. 5, 1821.
G. W. Gardenhire, BM. (CA, HRC)
John Ingleton to Betsey Poor, Oct. 26, 1821.
Pleasant Gilbert, BM. (Oct. 27, 1821) (CA)
George Irwin to Nancy Eldridge, Sep. 13, 1821.
Michael Anderson, BM. (CA)
William Jolly to Nancy Deatherage (or Etheridge), Dec. 11,
1821. Samuel Barnard, BM. (CA, HRC)
Stephen Killingsworth (or Killingsmith) to Nancy Hart,
Dec. 17, 1821. (Dec. 18, 1821) (CA, HRC)
Jacob Lacetter (or Loutten) to Martha Haley, Dec. 14, 1821.
Thomas Brown, BM. (Dec. 11, 1821) (CA)
Wm. Leftwock to Ann Moore, Dec. 17, 1821.
(Dec. 17, 1821) (CA)
Jesse Matlock to Elinor McPherson, Apr. 5, 1821.
Thos. Littleton, BM. (CA)
Thomas McGuire to Milly Stout, Dec. 6, 1821.
Anthony S. Dicky, BM. (Dec. 6, 1821) (CA)

30

Robert McHenry to Patsey Highton, Mar. 30, 1821.
   Samuel Anarew, BM. (CA)
Eli McNabb to Betsey Carson, Apr. 29, 1821.
   Daniel Wester, BM. (CA)
Thomas McNabb to Betsey Poor, May 5, 1821.
   Ethelridge Taylor, BM. (HRC)
Nathan McNatt to Polly Wester, Nov. 3, 1821.
   (Nov. 5, 1821) (CA)
Daniel Mizell to Nancy Evans, Mar. 17, 1821.
   Robert Moore, BM. (Mar 22, 1821) (CA)
Kader Mizell (or Meayles) to Mary McCormick, Apr. 9, 1821.
   Oswell Phillips, BM. (Apr. 9, 1821) (CA, HRC)
James Monds to Polly Williams, Aug. 3, 1821.
   William Williams, BM. (Aug. 5, 1821) (CA, HRC)
Edward T. Morgan to Letitia Allison, Nov. 17, 1821.
   Gideon Morgan, BM. (Dec. 17, 1821) (CA)
John Nail to Amy Watson, Oct. 16, 1821.
   John Stubb, BM. (CA)
William Nichone(?) to Elizabeth Breazeale, Mar. 3, 1821.
   (Mar. 5, 1821) (CA)
Nathan Paget to Kiziah Allen, Feb. 8, 1821.
   (HRC)
James Philpot to Delilah York, Apr. 30, 1821.
   Richard Philpot, BM. (CA)
Thomas Prater to Juda Browder, Sep. 12, 1821.
   Josiah Jackson, BM. (Sep. 13, 1821) (CA)
William Pritchett to Viney Keener, Jan. 30, 1821.
   Philip Pritchett, BM. (Jan. 30, 1821) (CA, HRC)
John Ray to Judy Webb, Dec. 26, 1821.
   Samuel Davis, BM. (CA)
Tandy Rice to Lindy Center, Dec. 25, 1821.
   James Crumbliss, BM. (Dec. 25, 1821) (CA)
John Riddle to Juda Easly, _____, 1821.
   Jonathan Harvey, BM. (HRC)
William Roberts to Zearbiah Roberts, Jan. 26, 1821.
   (Jan. 30, 1821) (CA)
Samuel Robinson to Malinda Powell, Oct. 29, 1821.
   Benjamin Hagwood, BM. (Nov. 1, 1821) (CA, HRC)
John Stewart to Nancy Givens, Oct. 20, 1821.
   (CA)
John (or James) Tedier to Elizabeth Todd, Feb. 21, 1821.
   Joseph Byrd, BM. (CA, HRC)
John Thompson to Nancy Recter, Nov. 28, 1821.
   Landon Rector, BM. (CA)
Asher Turner to Jane Carmichael, Oct. 25, 1821.
   Nathan Turner, BM. (Nov. 12, 1821) (CA)
Daniel Vann (or Vance) to Polly McComb, Jan. 16, 1821.
   Howard Utley, BM. (Jan. 18, 1821) (CA, HRC)
Audley P. Walker to Polly Noel, May 21, 1821.
   _____ Walker, William McKamey, BM. (HRC)
James Wilkerson to Lucy Rice, Sep. 5, 1821.
   (CA)
Sterling Williams to Polly Cobb, July 20, 1821.
   Asa Cobb, BM. (CA)

Thos. Williams to Betsey Kimbrell, Feb. 10, 1821.
   (Feb. 15, 1821) (CA)
Peter Wilson to Ann Shaw (or Shain), Dec. 1, 1821.
   Uriah Allison, BM. (Dec. 2, 1821) (CA)
William Wilson to Jenny Kimbrell (or Kimbull), Apr. 13,
   1821. Willis (or William) Crow, BM. (CA, HRC)

1822

Cornelius Acord, Jr. to Sarah Stewart (or Steward),
   Jan. 8, 1822. Cornelius Acord, Sr., BM. (Jan. 10, 1822)
   (CA)
David Acord to Elizabeth Hartley, _____, 1822.
   Cornelius Acord, BM. (CA)
Archibald Adcock to Rebeca Holland, June 1, 1822.
   Hugh Dunlap, William Lawson, BM. (CA)
Covington Allen to Creesy Acord, Feb. 8, 1822.
   (Feb. 6, 1822) (CA)
Abel Armstrong to Tabitha Rowton, May 1, 1822.
   (May 1, 1822) (CA)
Leonard Asher to Polly Clift, Apr. 14, 1822.
   Charles Asher, BM. (HRC)
Jacob Bassenger(?) to Elizabeth Dunn, May 16, 1822.
   (May 16, 1822) (CA)
John Belew to Kitty Melton, Jan. 16, 1822.
   Ambrose Copeland, BM. (Dec. 17, 1822) (CA)
William W. Berry to R. Caroline Meridith, Nov. 26, 1822.
   (Nov. 28, 1822) (CA)
William G. Black to Elizabeth McKinney, Aug. 20, 1822.
   (CA)
William W. Bomar to Miriah Merdith, Jan. 23, 1822.
   Addeson Carrack, BM. (Jan. 24, 1822) (CA)
William Branham to Catherine Goldsby, Dec. 18, 1822.
   (Dec. 22, 1822) (CA)
William Branham to Nancy Phillips, Jan. 12, 1822.
   (Jan. 12, 1822) (CA)
Livingston Brannen (or Branum) to Susannah Mead, Oct. 29,
   1822. John Eblen, BM. (Oct. 30, 1822) (CA)
John Breeden to Mary Forrester, May 10, 1822.
   (CA)
Hercules Buchanan to Clarka Taylor, Apr. 11, 1822.
   John Taylor, BM (Apr. 11, 1822) (CA)
Stephen Burris to Susanna Francis, Jan. 21, 1822.
   Mathew Miller, BM. (CA)
Joshua Cooly to Sally Rayburn, Aug. 10, 1822.
   William Bailey, BM. (CA)
James Dalton to Rhody Butler, Oct. 29, 1822.
   Robert Gilliland, BM. (Nov. 10, 1822) (CA)
Martin Durrett to Rebecca W. White, Sep. 10, 1822.
   Alexander Nesmith, James Robinson, BM. (Sep. 10, 1822)
   See also Martin Durret, 1818. (CA)
Peter Easter to Peggy Tate, Sep. 25, 1822.
   (Oct. 4, 1822) (CA)
Joshua Eaton to Mahala Holland, Mar. 20, 1822.
   Tyra Adcock, BM. (CA)

William Edwards to Polly Parks, Sep. 9, 1822.
James Parks, BM. (Nov. 12, 1822) (CA, HRC)
William Ellis to Margaret Mahan, Dec. 28, 1822.
George Green, BM. (Jan. 2, 1823) (CA)
William Enoss (or Inness or Eness) to Polly Burnett,
May 3, 1822. (May 5, 1822) (CA)
Joseph Ewing to Mary Cardwell, Sep. 20, 1822.
William Holland, BM. (CA)
Henry Fleener to Abigal Hunds, Aug. 7, 1822.
Joel Long, BM. (Aug. 14, 1822) (CA)
Harris B. Gallaher to Ciely Hatfield, Dec. 2, 1822.
David Ally, BM. (CA)
William Gay to Curly Gay, Oct. 3, 1822.
(Oct. 4, 1822) (CA)
John Goddard to Mary Fike, Dec. 20, 1822.
Josiah Fike, BM. (Dec. 12, 1822) (CA)
Nehimah Gresham to Polly Clark, June 15, 1822.
Philip Stephens, BM. (June 20, 1822) (CA, HRC)
Albert Hart (or Hurt) to Sally Garrett, May 14, 1822.
(CA)
Albert Henderson to Elizabeth Hawks, Aug. 16, 1822.
(Aug. 17, 1822) (CA)
James Hensley to Anna Ervin, Oct. 3, 1822.
John Melton, Meshac Green, BM. (CA)
James Hill to Patsey Taylor, Oct. 12, 1822.
Robert Marney, BM. (Oct. 15, 1822) (CA)
Stephen Huse to Betsey Hamblet, Aug. 12, 1822.
Elijah Rowden, William Hamblet, BM. (CA)
David Ingram to Hannah Erwin, Sep. 9, 1822.
Gastand Ingram, BM. (CA)
Henry Jolly to Polly McCollum, Nov. 28, 1822.
E. D. Taylor, William Jolly, BM. (Dec. 5, 1822)
(CA, HRC)
Hanton Lawson to Lucinda Hood, May 3, 1822.
(May 7, 1822) (CA)
John Longacre to Phebe P. Thorlton, Dec. 27, 1822.
Benjamin Longacre, BM. (Jan. 2, 1822) (CA)
Manuel McInturf to Nancy Hurt, Mar. 7, 1822.
(Mar. 7, 1822) (CA)
William McMead to Elizabeth Newman, Nov. 21, 1822.
John Loyd, William R. Lenoir, BM. (Nov. 21, 1822) (CA)
Jesse McPherson to Barbary Daugherty, Feb. 25, 1822.
(Feb. 25, 1822) (CA)
Richard McPherson to Mary Hazen, Jan. 27, 1822.
James McPherson, BM. (CA)
Spencer McPherson to Catherine McDuffy, Sep. 21, 1822.
Charles White, BM. (CA)
Joseph Moss to Betsey Ellis, _____, 1822.
Levi Wheat, BM. (CA)
Henry Newman to Sally Breazeale, Dec. (or Nov.) 10, 1822.
David R. Breazeale, BM. (Dec. 15, 1822) (CA, HRC)
Lewis Patterson to Polly Y. Person (or Parson), May 29,
1822. Abel Parson, BM. (May 30, 1822) (CA)
Robert H. Prine to Elizabeth Wroe, June 30, 1822.
(June 2(?), 1822) (CA)

Andrew Pritchett to Elizabeth Essary, May 2, 1822.
  (May 3, 1822) (CA)
George Reynolds to Betsey Rentfroe, Aug. 13, 1822.
  _____ Stephens, BM. (CA)
John A. Rice to Polly Hughlin (or Hughes), Feb. 27, 1822.
  (Feb. 28, 1822) (CA, HRC)
Robert Rice to Asha Stubbs, Feb. 4, 1822.
  (Feb. 28, 1822) (CA)
Isa Richards to Delila Right, Nov. 21, 1822.
  (Nov. 21, 1822) (CA)
John Riddle to Judy Easely, _____, 1822.
  Jonathan Harvey, BM. (CA)
John Selbe to Barbara Cook, Feb. 26, 1822.
  William Selbe, BM. (Feb. 26, 1822) (CA)
Isaac Sellers to Nancy Todd, Oct. 22, 1822.
  (HRC)
Henry Sutter (or Sullin) to Betsey Bucknel (or Becknal),
  July 11, 1822. Henry Bucknel, BM. (July 20, 1822) (CA)
Isaac Tate to Jane Randall, May 20, 1822.
  John Snow, BM. (June 2, 1822) (CA)
Andrew Turner to Polly McKain, Mar. 8, 1822.
  Abraham Bogart, BM. (Mar. 14, 1822) (CA)
John Underwood to Cintha Bandy(?), Dec. 17, 1822.
  (Dec. 17, 1822) (CA)

1823

Joseph Acord to Sally Stout, July 8, 1823.
  Samuel Waddy, BM. (July 10, 1823) (CA)
Jesse Averett to Elizabeth Davis, Apr. 20, 1823.
  Asa Davis, BM. (CA)
Hyram Berry (or Barry) to Nancy Eblen, Jan. 23, 1823.
  (Jan. 23, 1823) (HRC)
John Bower to Nancy Morgan, Sep. 9, 1823.
  John Crow, BM. (CA, HRC)
Adam Brandon to Rachel Rowden, June 18, 1823.
  Philip Brandon, BM. (CA)
Loman(?) Brasher to Rachel Roberts, Nov. 28, 1823.
  (Dec. 2, 1823) (CA)
George W. Bryan to Lucinda G. Collier, Oct. 25, 1823.
  (Oct. 30, 1823) (CA)
Thomas Butler to Elizabeth Gammon, Nov. 4, 1823.
  Jacob Butler, BM. (CA)
Jesse Carter to Betsey Sutton, Nov. 6, 1823.
  (Nov. 20, 1823) (CA)
Francis K. Center to Nancy A. Gallaher, Dec. 17, 1823.
  Hugh L. Breazeale, BM. (Dec. 23, 1823) (CA)
William S. Cook to Rachel Roberts, June 7, 1823.
  Alexander Nesmith, Alexander Nail, BM. (CA)
James Cooly to Rebecca Cooley, Dec. 20, 1823.
  William Carroll, BM. (Dec. 21, 1823) (CA)
Solomon Copland to Jane Harrison, Dec. 15, 1823.
  John Murrah, BM. (CA)
Howard L. Council to Lucinda Gallaher, Mar. 10, 1823.
  James A. Gallaher, BM. (CA)

Benjamin L. Cross (or Crow) to Betty Sutton, Aug. 19, 1823.
John Crow, BM. (Aug. 23, 1823) (CA, HRC)
Alexander Crow to Nancy Dugger, Dec. 3, 1823.
John Bowers, BM. (Dec. 4, 1823) (CA)
Abner Deatherage to Rebecca Davis, Nov. 25, 1823.
John M. Hale, BM. (HRC)
John Dover to Elizabeth Moore, Nov. 15, 1823.
(Nov. 16, 1823) (CA)
Fredrick Early to Nancy _____, May 10, 1823.
Thomas Early, Francis Ellis, BM. (CA)
Jefferson Eldridge to Rachel Blair, July 22, 1823.
Jesse Eldridge, BM. (July 24, 1823) (CA)
John Elkins to Nancy Waren, July 30, 1823.
Jacob Waren, BM. (CA)
William Erwin to Polly Roberts, May 14, 1823.
(May 15, 1823) (CA)
James Ewin to Sarah Levi, July 4, 1823.
John Molton, BM. (CA)
Jacob Ewing to Anna Matheny, Oct. 4, 1823.
Arthur Ewing, BM. (CA)
Thomas Farman to Rachel Murrey, Nov. 3, 1823.
Edward Roberts, BM. (HRC)
Abraham Fleener(?) to Polly Thompson, Aug. 16, 1823.
Robert Cooper, BM. (Aug. 17, 1823) (CA)
Larkin Forrester to Sarah Tuten, Oct. 28, 1823.
Wiley Tuton, BM. (Oct. 28, 1823) (CA, HRC)
George Gallaher to Amanda Williams, Dec. 8, 1823.
Thomas Gallaher, BM. (Dec. 11, 1823) (CA)
Thomas Gallaher to Amelia Williams, Aug. 3 (or 30), 1823.
Joseph Byrd, William Carroll, BM. (CA, HRC)
James Gallaway to Catherine Walker, Apr. 16, 1823.
Levi Galloway, BM. (Apr. 17, 1823) (CA)
Shedrick Gibson to Rebecca Ballard, May 23, 1823.
George Moore, BM. (CA)
William Hail to Elizabeth Francis, Feb. 24, 1823.
C. McKamy, BM. (Mar. 2, 1823) (CA)
John Hamlet to Jane White, Dec. 15, 1823.
William Hamlet, BM. (Dec. 17, 1823) (CA)
William Hankins to Candis Yearls, Aug. 2, 1823.
Thomas Hankins, BM. (CA)
Samuel Harwell to Sophia E. Ayer, Oct. 21, 1823.
John M. Breazeale, BM. (Oct. 23, 1823) (CA, HRC)
Eli Hellunes to Jane Hope, Aug. 16, 1823.
(Aug. 21, 1823) (CA)
Isaac Hembree to Mary Blake, Nov. 12, 1823.
Joseph M. Clark, BM. (HRC)
Jonathan Hendrix to Agnes Branham, June 19, 1823.
Matthews Williams, BM. (June 19, 1823) (CA)
James Hunt to Patsey Hays, Dec. 20, 1823.
(Dec. 20, 1823) (CA)
Sanford Ingram to Polly Burnett, May 8, 1823.
(May 12, 1823) (CA)
John Jones to Susan Flenner, Oct. 7, 1823.
William P. Smith, BM. (CA)

John Lane to Lilly Highton, Jan. 29, 1823.
 Solomon Stow, BM. (Dec. 31, 1823) (CA)
Thomas Lane to Judy Robison (or Robinson), June 5, 1823.
 (CA, HRC)
Lewallin Lewis to Michael Taylor, Jan. 11, 1823.
 (Jan. 16, 1823) (CA)
Thomas Liles to Polly Russoll, Feb. 25, 1823.
 (Feb. 27, 1823) (CA)
Jonathan Luster to Eliza Willis, July 28, 1823.
 Samuel S. Walker, BM. (July 29, 1823) (CA)
William Lyles (or Syler) to Charlotte Foute, Apr. 8, 1823.
 John Purris, BM. (Apr. 8, 1823) (CA)
Jesse Mainard to Ruthy Clark, Feb. 4, 1823.
 (Feb. 6, 1823) (CA)
William B. Marshal to Nancy Redmon, June 18, 1823.
 Benjamin Redmon, BM. (CA)
James W. McCabb to Susannah Hope, Oct. 20, 1823.
 Evan Evans, BM. (CA)
Alexander McDaniel to Sally Jones, Aug. 29, 1823.
 John Moore, BM. (CA)
Garland Moore to Alice Lamb, Aug. 5, 1823.
 John Moore, BM. (CA)
Joshua Moore to Mossy Ann Childress, Dec. 8, 1823.
 Thomas C. Wroe, BM. (Dec. 11, 1823) (CA)
Alex Nexmith to Nancy Roberts, Nov. 11, 1823.
 George W. Gardenhire, BM. (Nov. 11, 1823) (CA)
Abraham Odel to Jane Jones, _____, 1823.
 John Jones, Brittain Mathews, BM. (CA)
Isaac Oliver to Betsey Patty, Sep. 13, 1823.
 John Hankins, BM. (CA)
Henry Penick to Susana Scisco, Aug. 12, 1823.
 (Aug. 12, 1823) (CA)
David Perkins to Polly Parine, July 7, 1823.
 Benjamin Longacre, Jr., BM. (July 9, 1823) (CA)
David M. Porter to Susan K. Dunlap, Oct. 8, 1823.
 John Wm. Breazeale, BM. (Oct. 23, 1823) (CA)
William Pursely to Patsey Gallion, Jan. 25, 1823.
 Abraham Gallion, BM. (Jan. 26, 1823) (CA)
William Rather to Milly Ezell, May 10, 1823.
 Woddy Thompson, BM. (May 11, 1823) (CA)
Benjamin Redmon to Martha Lewallen, _____, 1823.
 Fergason Redmon, BM. (CA)
Francis Rhea to Billinda Longacre, June 21, 1823.
 John Montgomery, BM. (June 22, 1823) (CA)
Isaac Rice to Susan Center, Dec. 17, 1823.
 (Dec. 18, ____) (CA)
William Roath to Lydia Elkins, Oct. 9, 1823.
 Jacob Warren, BM. (HRC)
John Roberts to Charity Johnson, Dec. 9, 1823.
 (Dec. 15, 1823) (CA)
Allen Rose to Mary Ault, Dec. 22, 1823.
 (Dec. 24, 1823) (CA)
John Sharp to Betsey Lower, Mar. 20, 1823.
 Thomas McKinney, BM. (Mar. 20, 1823) (CA)

James H. Smith to Milly Stout, Apr. 19, 1823.
  Joseph Acord, Daniel Wester, BM. (CA)
William Sutton to Rayne Clemmons, Sep. 2 (or 20), 1823.
  James Raynold, BM. (Oct. 3, 1823) (CA, HRC)
Richard H. Talifaro (or Taliaferro) to Elizabeth Ballard,
  Apr. 20, 1823. (May 1, 1823) (CA)
Thomas Tannon to Rachel Murray, Nov. 27, 1823.
  (Nov. 28, 1823) (CA)
Waddy Thompson to Patsey Byrdwell, Feb. 5, 1823.
  Thomas Cox, BM. (Feb. 6, 1823) (CA, HRC)
Jonathan Underwood to Polly Staton, Apr. 29, 1823.
  John McKamy, BM. (May 1, 1823) (CA, HRC)
Henry Wilkins to Sally Lyle, July 31, 1823.
  John Brown, BM. (Aug. 5, 1823) (CA)
William Wilkinson to Sally Tyler, July 31, 1823.
  John Brown, BM. (HRC)
John Windle to Polly Hunter, Aug. 20, 1823.
  Isaac Johnson, BM. (Sep. 4, 1823) (CA, HRC)
Joseph York to Sarah Blake, Nov. 10, 1823.
  Thos. Blake, BM. (CA)

1824

Henson Allison to Jane Casey, Mar. 27, 1824.
  Levi Casey, BM. (CA)
Michael Anderson to Patsey Pritchett, Dec. 30, 1824.
  Joseph Hankins, BM. (Dec. 31, 1825) (CA)
James Ausbern to Fanny Smith, Jan. 7, 1824.
  (Jan. 8, 1824) (CA)
Jacob Baker to Gracy McCain, Feb. 18, 1824.
  (Feb. 19, 1824) (CA, HRC)
George Blackwell to Alsey (or Olsey) Martin, Jan. 27 (or
  29), 1824. Burwele Tanner, BM. (Jan. 29, 1824) (CA, HRC)
Richard Blackwell to Tamer Martin, Mar. 25, 1824.
  Burwele Tanner, BM. (Mar. 25, 1824) (CA)
Jefferson Branan to Rosy Grantan, Oct. 28, 1824.
  Edward Culvehouse, BM. (CA)
Adam Brandon to Rachel Rowden, June 18, 1824.
  Phillip Brandon, BM. (HRC)
Robert H. Brazeale to Anna McKamy, Apr. 11, 1824.
  J. W. M. Brazeale, BM. (HRC)
John Wm. Breazeale to Betty Margrave, Feb. 5, 1824.
  Addison Carrick, BM. (Feb. 5, 1824) (CA, HRC)
Joseph Brittain to Ruthy Parker, Mar. 4 (or 18), 1824.
  Able Jackson, BM. (Mar. __, 1824) (CA)
Milton Burk to Phebe Hatley, Jan. 24, 1824.
  Lewis Renfro, BM. (HRC)
William Bussle to Judy Johnson, Aug. 19, 1824.
  Francis Benton, BM. (CA)
William Clift to Mary Penland, Mar. 4, 1824.
  (HRC)
James Crew to Anna Lawson, July 17, 1824.
  (HRC)
Valentine Cunningham to Elizabeth Howard, May 26, 1824.
  Samuel Selbe, BM. (CA)

John Daniel to _____ Allison, Sep. 2, 1824.
  Wiley Tuton, BM. (CA)
Edward Davis to Polly Underwood, Dec. 9, 1824.
  Samuel C. Davis, BM. (CA)
John Davis to Nancy Ginkins, Dec. 21, 1824.
  Moore Matlock, BM. (Dec. 21, 1824) (CA)
Byrd Deatheridge, Jr. to Alsy Man, Oct. 6, 1824.
  Philip Rushan, BM. (CA)
George Decker to Jane Branham, Nov. 12, 1824.
  Phillip Huff, BM. (HRC)
Fountaine Dotson to Polly Parker, July 27, 1824.
  James Parker, BM. (CA)
Benjamine Dunkin to Jane Hannah, June 1, 1824.
  William G. Blake, BM. (HRC)
Willis Evans to Rebecca Shadrick (or Shadwick), Nov. 8,
  1824. William Kane, BM. (Nov. 11, 1824) (CA, HRC)
John Fifer (or Tifer) to Ellinor Morgan, Nov. 16, 1824.
  Samuel Nave, BM. (May 25, 1825) (CA)
George Findly to Jane Spence, Mar. 8, 1824.
  (Mar. 11, 1824) (CA)
Samuel Finley to Elizabeth E. Collier, Jan. 29, 1824.
  Wm. Bryan, BM. (CA)
William D. Fout to Mary Williams, Feb. 7, 1824.
  William Williams, BM. (CA)
James Freeman to Axey Pander, Oct. 17, 1824.
  Daniel Huffine, BM. (CA)
Jonathan Gibson to Susan Rector, Nov. 3, 1824.
  Noah Ashley, BM. (CA)
Jacob (F?) Hendrick (or Kindrick) to Margaret McPherson,
  Nov. 27, 1824. Allen Haley, BM. (Nov. 24, 1824) (CA, HRC)
James Lackey to Jane Matlock, Nov. 6, 1824.
  (Nov. 9, 1824) (CA, HRC)
Ralph Lane to Mary Williams, Aug. 26, 1824.
  James Killingsworth, BM. (CA)
Samuel Lane to Milly Robinson, June 22 (or 26), 1824.
  (Jan. 26, 1824) (CA, HRC)
Benton Lanston to Betsy Haskins, July 21 (or 31), 1824.
  James Harris (or Harrison), BM. (Aug. 1, 1824) (CA)
John Lemmons, Jr. to Elizabeth Burnett, Dec. 13, 1824.
  (Dec. 16, 1824) (CA)
Larkin Lewis to Sally Jinkins, June 28, 1824.
  David Lewis, BM. (CA)
Jesse Lowe to Prudance England, Jan. 22 (or 27), 1824.
  Chas. Thompson, BM. (CA, HRC)
Joseph Lyle to Nancy Cofer, July 16, 1824.
  Thos. Cox, BM. (July 18, 1824) (CA, HRC)
Isaac Matlock to Jane Selvidge, Mar. 1 (or 10), 1824.
  (Mar. 10, 1824) (CA, HRC)
William McAlester to Abigail Bell, Nov. 27, 1824.
  Henry Bogart, BM. (CA)
Robert McHenry to Patsy Hightower, Mar. 30, 1824.
  Samuel Andrews, BM. (HRC)
William McKain to Elizabeth Breazeale, Mar. 3, 1824.
  Jacob Baker, BM. See also William Nickland, 1824) (CA)

John Mee to Sarah McElwee, Feb. 4 (or 11), 1824.
    Addison Carrick, BM. (Feb. 12, 1824) (CA, HRC)
William Montgomery to Betsey Winten, Mar. 11, 1824.
    (Apr. 2, 1824) (CA)
Joseph Moore to Polly Y_____, Sep. 28, 1824.
    George Moore, BM. (CA)
Richard Moorehead to Polly Berry, Aug. 15, 1824.
    (CA, HRC)
Henry More to Elizabeth Anthony, Jan. 14, 1824.
    (Jan. 15, 1824) (CA)
Pulaski Nelson to Mariana Hall, Feb. 24, 1824.
    Zachariah Hall, BM. (CA)
John Nesmith to Phebe Roberts, Jan. 2, 1824.
    Wm. McKamy, BM. (CA, HRC)
William Nickland to Elizabeth Brazeale, Mar. 5, 1824.
    See also William McKain. (HRC)
Abraham Odum to Sally Henderson, Sep. 6, 1824.
    Alex Forrester, William McKamey, BM. (HRC)
George Preston to Elizabeth Parmerly, Apr. 7, 1824.
    James Preston, BM. (CA)
Phillip Prititch to Charity Etheridge, Dec. 30, 1824.
    Peter Manning, BM. (HRC)
Devircaux(?) Rather to Eliza Cole, Dec. 29, 1824.
    Wiley Tuton, BM. (Jan. 2, 1825) (CA)
James Rather to Elizabeth Wheat, Sep. 18, 1824.
    John Rather, BM. (CA)
Richard Reves (or Reeves) to Eliza Miller, Jan. 15 (or
    25), 1824. Mathias Miller, BM. (Dec. 25, 1824) (CA, HRC)
William Rose to Peggy Ault, Apr. 11, 1824.
    Solomon Wilkins, BM. (CA)
William Sawords to Mary Manning, Nov. 4, 1824.
    Peter Manning, BM. (HRC)
John Smith to S_____ McGomery, Oct. 5, 1824.
    Elish (Elisha?) Ginkins, BM. (CA)
Andrew Staples to Sally Kimbreal, Dec. 25, 1824.
    (Dec. 30, 1824) (CA)
John Taliaferro to Martha Wright, May 25, 1824.
    W. C. Dunlap, BM. (May 26, 1824) (CA)
James H. Temple to Mary E. Alexander, Nov. 20, 1824.
    (Nov. 23, 1824) (CA)
Elisha Turner to Jane Ward, Nov. 1, 1824.
    John Woody, BM. (CA)
John B. Waller to Catherine Pickel, Oct. 4, 1824.
    (Oct. 5, 1824) (CA)
John Wheat to Nancy Rather, Jan. 21 (or 24), 1824.
    Levi Wheat, BM. (CA, HRC)
Francis Wood to Polly Burk, Feb. 15, 1824.
    Caleb Wood, BM. (CA)
Christopher Woods to Ellinor Easter, May 29, 1824.
    William D. Miller, BM. (Mar. 4, 1824) (CA)
John Woody to Elizabeth Farmer, Jan. 28, 1824.
    (Jan. 29, 1824) (CA, HRC)
George Wroe to Nancy Funk, Aug. 18, 1824.
    (Aug. 19, 1824) (CA)

John Adams to Polly Miller, Mar. 14 (or 15), 1825.
Washington Hudson, BM. (CA)
Francis Aldridg to Susan Bellard, Feb. 19, 1825.
(Apr. 1, 1825) (CA)
Michael Anderson to Patsy Pritchett, Dec. 30, 1825.
(HRC)
William Anderson to Eliza M. E. McEwen, Sep. 6, 1825.
(HRC)
William Andrew to Mary Raybourn, Sep. 6, 1825.
Isaac Barger, BM. (Sep. 6, 1825) (CA)
Washington Bacon to Eliza Miller, June 8, 1825.
(June 8, 1825) (CA)
Allen Battam (or Bolton) to Margaret Gardenhire, June 25,
1825. William Harvey, BM. (June 28, 1825) (CA, HRC)
Esquire Bedwell to Sally West, Oct. 20, 1825.
Hiram Bedwell, BM. (CA)
Thomas Bell to Polly McNight, Apr. 8, 1825.
James Buckhannon, BM. (Apr. 8, 1825) (CA, HRC)
William S. Boake to Rachel Roberts, June 9, 1825.
(June 10, 1825) (CA)
Henry Bogart to Polly Woody, Aug. 22, 1825.
Abraham Bogart, BM. (CA)
George Bowman to Nancy Browder, Oct. 29, 1825.
See also George Branan, 1825. (HRC)
George Branan to Nancy Branan, Oct. 29, 1825.
Derians Browder, BM. See also George Bowman, 1825.
(Oct. 29, 1825) (CA)
Samuel Brown to Betsey Morgan, Mar. 28, 1825.
Washington Hudson, BM. (CA)
Lewis Burris to Nancy Francis, Apr. 16, 1825.
William Hale, BM. (Apr. 16, 1825) (CA)
Moses Caps to Dicy Cane, Aug. 28, 1825.
William Cane, BM. (Aug. 29, 1825) (CA, HRC)
Marcus Carter to Susana Carter, Aug. 15, 1825.
Ephraim Cate, BM. (CA)
Gilbert Christian to Moly Terry, Oct. 27, 1825.
Jonah Terry, BM. (Oct. 27, 1825) (CA)
John Gravet to Penelope Tilly, June 17, 1825.
Oxley Johnson, Robert Clough, BM. (CA)
Robert Crow to Polly Cox, Sep. 23, 1825.
Hugh Francis, BM. (CA)
John Davis to Francis Duncan, Feb. 18 (or May 17), 1825.
(May 18, 1825) (CA, HRC)
William Eblen to Lucretia Smith, Sep. 14, 1825.
Wm. M. McCowin, BM. (Sep. 14, 1825) (CA)
Rubin Evans to Rebecca Lanston (or Lauston), Oct. 5, 1825.
Daniel Mizell, BM. (Oct. 5, 1825) (CA, HRC)
Abraham Foshee to Thankful Rice, Aug. 18, 1825.
(Aug. 18, 1825) (CA)
Hugh Francis to Sally Cox, Apr. 8, 1825.
Lewis Burris, BM. (Apr. 8, 1825) (CA)
George Fritts to Usley Blevins, Dec. 9, 1825.
Henry Fritts, Absolum Miller, BM. (Dec. 11, 1825) (CA)

ROANE COUNTY MARRIAGES

Peter Fritz to Permelia (or Parmelia) Williams, Dec. 24
(or 25), 1825. Isaac Bargor, BM. (CA, HRC)
Abraham Galyon to Patsey Parker, Nov. 26, 1825.
(Nov. 27, 1825) (CA)
Richard Gray to Sarah Brown, Sep. 5, 1825.
Uriah Allison, BM. (CA)
David Haley to Betsy Fleiner, Oct. 29, 1825.
(HRC)
Preston Hankins to Jane Glass, Sep. 5, 1825.
Stephen Lawson, BM. (CA)
John Hostler (or Haster) to Elizabeth Dow (or Dore),
July 13, 1825. (July 13, 1825) (CA, HRC)
John Haynis (or Hanis) to Elizabeth Hider, Dec. 12, 1825.
James I. Hanes, BM. (CA)
James R. Hines to Rachel Abeel, Oct. 5, 1825.
John Hamilton, BM. (HRC)
William A. Hodge to Lydea Breeden, June 10, 1825.
(June 10, 1825) (CA)
William Littleton to Martha Brahen, Aug. 11, 1825.
John Tammins(?), BM. (CA)
Backster McKnight to Mary Rodgers, Dec. 28, 1825.
James Rogers, BM. (CA)
William Maddox to Elizabeth Pearkin, Aug. 5, 1825.
Benj. H. Gallaher, BM. (CA)
William T. Maden to Eliza M. E. McEwin, May 24, 1825.
D. G. Dunlap, BM. (May 24, 1825) (CA)
Moore Matlock to Rebecca Pickel, Mar. 5, 1825.
John Hope, BM. (CA)
William McDaniel to Nancy Soward, July 22, 1825.
Peter Manning, BM. (Aug. 2, 1825) (CA)
Robert McNutt to Nancy Etheridge (or Eldridge), June 8,
1825. Larkin Forester, BM. (CA, HRC)
Thomas McNutt to Agness Solomon, Jan. 11, 1825.
John E. Nelson, Thomas Nelson, BM. (Jan. 15, 1825)
(CA, HRC)
William McNutt to Sarah Weese (or Weiss), Jan. 3, 1825.
Wiley Luten, BM. (CA, HRC)
Samuel Miles to Jincy Collins, Mar. 10, 1825.
Shadrick Gentry, John Scott, BM. (CA)
Hiram Miller to Ally McCollom, Feb. 23, 1825.
(Feb. 24, 1825) (CA)
Julius Mount to Polly Davis, Sep. 25, 1825.
_____ Silvey, BM. (Sep. 25, 1822(?) (CA)
William Musgrove to Nancy Daniel, Feb. 15, 1825.
Richard Richards, BM. (CA)
William New to Martha Barrow, Aug. 27, 1825.
Robert Cannon, BM. (Aug. 31, 1825) (CA)
Nathaniel Osburn to Rebecca Tuten, June 20, 1825.
Richard Richards, BM. (CA)
John Pearson to Mary Medans, Aug. 17, 1825.
William Branham, BM. (CA)
Richard Pepper to Dicy Hogg, Oct. 7, 1825.
(Oct. 25, 1825) (CA)
Peter Perry to Barbary Ann Bonds, Nov. 30, 1825.
Edward Pritchett, BM. (HRC)

Jacob Phillips to Jane Miller, July 25, 1825.
(Aug. 2, 1825) (CA, HRC)
William D. Phillips to Susan B. Clark, Oct. 27, 1825.
William Lyons, BM. (CA, HRC)
Elias Riddle to Elizabeth McClelan, Dec. 5, 1825.
Daniel Higgins, BM. (CA)
Jacob Rinkle to Levicy Webb, Dec. 14, 1825.
Hiriam Johnson, BM. (Dec. 18, 1825) (CA, HRC)
Jesse M. Roberts to Jane Lacy, Aug. 24, 1825.
Benj. Taliaferro, BM. (CA)
James Rogers to Elinor Russle, Feb. 1, 1825.
Robert Lyle, BM. (Feb. 1, 1825) See James Russell,
1825. (CA)
Elkanah Roudon to Catherine M. Kody, Feb. 7, 1825.
(CA)
Abraham Rowden to Ann Brandon, Sep. 26, 1825.
Adam Brandon, BM. (HRC)
James Russell to Elendor Russell, Feb. __, 1825.
See James Rogers, 1825. (HRC)
Branton Sams to Susannah Casey, Apr. 23, 1825.
(Apr. 26, 1825) (CA)
Jacob Scrogains to Margaret McPherson, Feb. 10, 1825.
Alexander McPherson, BM. (CA)
Joseph Seales to Elizabeth Blair, Dec. 26, 1825.
John Blair, BM. (Dec. 27, 1825) (CA)
James H. Smith to Milly Stout, Apr. 19, 1825.
(Apr. 20, 1825) (CA)
Robert Stow to Mary Littleton, Sep. 20, 1825.
Lewis Gordan, BM. (Sep. 10, 1825) (CA)
William Sutian (or Sexton) to Susan Penick, Dec. 15, 1825.
(Dec. 15, 1825) (CA, HRC)
Thos. B. Swan to Margaret H. Cravens, Mar. 17, 1825.
John Maddon, BM. (CA)
Sherod A. Tallant to Barbary Smith, June 1, 1825.
Stephen West, Robert Crow, BM. (CA)
James J. Vess (or Vest) to Susan Witts, Aug. 11, 1825.
Wiley Tuton, BM. (CA)
John Wallace to Eliza H. McCawl (or McCowl), Feb. 24, 1825.
J. H. Jordain, BM. (CA, HRC)
Carr Waller to Keziah Eblen, May 6, 1825.
John B. Waller, BM. (CA)
David White to Catherine Davis, Mar. 17, 1825.
Lewis W. Jordan, BM. (CA)
Joseph White to Sally Thralekill, Dec. 29, 1825.
(Jan. 4, 1826) (CA)
Mathew Williams to Rebecca Doaisan(?), Nov. 21, 1825.
(Nov. 21, 1825) (CA)
Jacob Winton to Jane Frazier, Sep. 27, 1825.
Elijah Skeene, BM. (CA)
William Young to Polly Alif, Nov. 29, 1825.
(HRC)

1826

Charles Adkins to Margaret T. McMinn, Dec. 28 (or 29),
  1826. James P. Haynes, BM. (CA, HRC)
William Booth to Eliza Littrel, Dec. 14, 1826.
  (HRC)
Elijah W. Breazeale to Nancy McMullin, Mar. 15, 1826.
  Benj. F. Breazeale, BM. (Mar. 15, 1826) (CA)
William Breazeale to Betsey Margrave, Feb. 5, 1826.
  Addison Carrick, BM. (CA)
Gidean Butler to Jane Stewart, Oct. 26, 1826.
  (Oct. 26, 1826) (CA)
Walter Butler to Elizabeth Gilbreath, July 20, 1826.
  (CA)
James Cane to Abigall Bell, Feb. 22, 1826.
  Moses Caps, BM. (CA)
Caleb Carter to Susan Carter(?), Aug. 15, 1826.
  Samuel Eskridge, Ephraim Cates, BM. (HRC)
Henry Davidson to Patsey Marney, June 1, 1826.
  William Davidson, BM. (CA)
Samuel Davis to Jane Smith, Jan. 26, 1826.
  Samuel Marney, BM. (Jan. 26, 1826) (CA)
William Day to Patsey (or Patty) Shahan, Sep. 28, 1826.
  George W. Sims, BM. (Oct. 1, 1826) (CA, HRC)
Benjamin Duncan to Jane Hannah, June 1, 1826.
  William G. Blake, BM. (CA)
Samuel Evans to Arty Lawson, Dec. 6, 1826.
  John _____, BM. (CA)
Edward (or Edmond) Ford to Pheby Butler, Sep. (or Feb.)
  11, 1826. Thomas Blake, BM. (CA, HRC)
James Ford to Anna Davis, Jan. 14, 1826.
  Brittain Davis, BM. (CA)
James Freeman to Axey Pander, Oct. 17, 1826.
  (Oct. 17, 1826) (CA)
James Gallaher to Jane Wiley, Apr. 4, 1826.
  Andrew Sawyer, BM. (HRC)
Isaac Gallyon to Nancy Johnson, Aug. 22, 1826.
  Benjamin Hensley, BM. (CA, HRC)
George Gardenhire to Mary Ballard, _____, 1826.
  Addeson Carrack, BM. (CA)
John Grinant (or Grinatt or Grunant) to Sally Bowman,
  Oct. 2, 1826. Samuel Bowman, BM. (CA, HRC)
John Gunning (or Gennings) to Jane Eaton, Sep. (or Dec.)
  12, 1826. William McPherson, BM. (Dec. 14, 1826)
  (CA, HRC)
Absolem Hicks to Creslina Matheny (or Cretora Molting),
  May 5, 1826. John Moore, BM. (May 8, 1826) (CA, HRC)
Joel Hood to Nancy Haskins, Mar. 14, 1826.
  Bejamin F. Breazeale, BM. (CA, HRC)
Adam Horner to Mary Hinds, Apr. 19, 1826.
  Silvanus Hans(?), BM. (Apr. 30, 1826) (CA)
Anderson Hyden to Margaret Wrinkle, Mar. 25, 1826.
  Lewis Bowman, BM. (CA)
Uriah Irick to Patsey Sharrin, Mar. 11, 1826.
  (Mar. ___, 1826) (CA)

Nathaniel Jarralt to Sarah T. Brown, Oct. 19, 1826.
John Brown, BM. (Oct. 19, 1826) (CA)
William Jones to Lydia Moore (or Moon), Sep. 6, 1826.
Jones Moore (or Moon), BM. (Sep. 7, 1826) (CA, HRC)
John Julan to Jane Taylor, Dec. 2, 1826.
Wentley Sturges, BM. (HRC)
Jim Kirnes(?) to Nancy Short, Mar. 23, 1826.
Samuel Cannon, BM. (CA)
Titas Lacey (or Telas Laney) to Malinda T. Hamilton (or
Hamelton), Jan. 3, 1826. Daniel Lancy, BM. (June 6,
1826) (CA, HRC)
Robert Love to Lucy Green, May 23, 1826.
F. H. Gregory, BM. (May 23, 1826) (CA)
John Mann to Delila Woody, Sep. 15, 1826.
(CA)
Robert Marney to Anne Stephenson, Feb. 23, 1826.
William Eblen, BM. (CA)
Alexander Mason to Polly Mason, Mar. 27, 1826.
James Carden, BM. (Mar. 27, 1826) (CA)
Hezekiah Miller to Ann Wiggons, Mar. 8 (or 9), 1826.
Absolom Watt (or West), BM. (CA, HRC)
Christopher Moats to Sarah Tallant, Sep. 29, 1826.
Lewis Bryant, BM. (CA)
Joseph Moore to Mary Turner, Sep. 28, 1826.
(Sep. 28, 1826) (CA)
Samuel Moore to Ann E. Parks, June 14, 1826.
(June 15, 1826) (CA)
B. L. Mullins to Beany Sharp, Sep. 1, 1826.
(CA)
John Oliver to Barbary McCrery, July 27, 1826.
John Hope, Lewis Bowman, William Weese, BM. (HRC)
Joseph Parks (or Parker) to Betsey Thrailkill, Jan. 24,
1826. Jonathan Underwood, BM. (Jan. 24, 1826) (CA, HRC)
Benjamine Pride to Catherine Wroe, Sep. 19, 1826.
(_____ 19, 1826) (CA)
William Prior to Sally Burnett, Dec. 16, 1826.
Samuel Dicky, BM. (CA)
John Rowden to Sally Paget, Aug. 1, 1826.
Elijah Rowden, BM. (CA)
William Smith to Mary Tennor, June 27, 1826.
Solomon Bogart, BM. (CA)
Joshua Soward to Mary Amos, Feb. 1, 1826.
Peter Manning, BM. (CA)
John Stubbs to Mariam Nail, Nov. 20, 1926.
John Nail, BM. (HRC)
John Stubb to Monann Nail, Nov. 2, 1826.
(CA)
Peter Sylor (or Tyler) to Sally Adaems, Sep. 20 (or 26),
1826. John Loyd, BM. (CA, HRC)
Mile Tuckson (or Luckjon) to Polly Huff, Mar. 11, 1826.
(Mar. 14, 1826) (CA, HRC)
Elisha Turner to Jane Ward, Nov. 1, 1826.
(HRC)
John Turner to Edy Wester, Feb. 10, 1826.
Arthur Ewin, BM. (CA)

William Walker to Patsey Cannon, Feb. 22, 1826.
Samuel Walker, BM. (CA)
James Wiseman to Polly Spind, Feb. 9, 1826.
Henry Liggett, BM. (Feb. 9, 1826) (CA, HRC)
William Yates to Elendor Cragen, Feb. 4, 1826.
Samuel Terry, BM. (Feb. 5, 1826) (CA)

1827

John M. Abels to Polly Pritchett, May 5, 1827.
Francis Able, BM. (May 6, 1827) (CA)
Alexander Adkison to Malinda Powell, Dec. 17, 1827.
John Powell, BM. (CA)
William Allen to Mary Killingsworth, Oct. 4, 1827.
Wiley Tuton, BM. (CA)
David Ambrose to Kisiah Rale (or Robb), Mar. 31, 1827.
(CA, HRC)
Aron Archer to Elizabeth Carroll, Dec. 18, 1827.
John Carmichael, BM. (Dec. 18, 1827) (CA)
William Berry to Lucy Ballard, Oct. 8, 1827.
William Ballard, BM. (CA)
John Blair to Betsey Johnson, Mar. 27, 1827.
John Carmichael, BM. (Mar. 29, 1827) (CA)
George Brandon to Priscilla Bryant, July 10, 1827.
John Montgomery, BM. (July 10, 1827) (CA)
Robert S. Breashur to Easther Dearmond, Nov. 3, 1827.
Michael Hostler, Samuel H. Jordan, BM. (CA)
John Browder to Minerva Matlock, Dec. 7, 1827.
(HRC)
William Brown to Polly Weese, Mar. 2, 1827.
(Mar. 20, 1827) (CA)
Isaac Burris to Nancy Morris, Feb. 8, 1827.
Linsey Tinel, BM. (CA)
Cornelius Carmicel to Sally Williams, Dec. 4, 1827.
(Dec. 4, 1827) (CA)
Thomas Carter to Elinor Walker, Jan. 16, 1827.
Robert Carter, BM. (CA)
Willis S. Center to Janey M. Gallaher, Sep. 17, 1827.
John B. Morrison, BM. (CA.)
William Clark to Eveline Taylor, Jan. 27, 1827.
Jesse Galloway, James Cofer, BM. (CA)
Henry Cluck to Ludy Wells, Sep. 7, 1827.
William Cluck, BM. (HRC)
Rubin Cook to Elizabeth Walker, Aug. 28, 1827.
John Pickel, BM. (CA)
James Crisp to Fanny Lamb, Sep. 21, 1827.
Samuel Walker, BM. (CA)
John Davidson to Sarah Hankins, July 26, 1827.
Alexander Ayers, BM. (HRC)
Thomas Donahua (or Donohoo) to Mariana (or Marian) Harris,
June 5, 1827. Thomas F. Harris, BM. (June 5, 1827)
(CA, HRC)
Jim Dotson to Sally Sharp, July 23, 1827.
Carington Allen, BM. (CA)

Andrew English to Sarah Rigg, Feb. 17, 1827.
Jonathan Henson, BM. (CA)
Levi Ezell to Polly Rather, Feb. 2, 1827.
William Rather, BM. (CA)
Stephen Fort, Sen. to Peggy West, Feb. 21, 1827.
Hezekiah Hotchkiss, BM. (HRC)
Abraham Gann to Polly McKinney, Apr. 17, 1827.
George Isly, BM. (CA)
Reuben Gibson to Mary Woodard, _____, 1827(?)
(HRC)
Alexander Gilbert to Susan Burk, July 27, 1827.
James Dalton, BM. (HRC)
Alexander Gilbreath to Peggy Snodgrass, June 23, 1827.
John B. Mason, BM. (HRC)
Robert S. Gilliland to Caroline Center, Jan. 21, 1827.
James Gamble, BM. (CA)
James Grammer to Susan Gravely (or McCulley), Jan. 23,
1827. Robert Tucker, BM. (Jan. 25, 1827) (CA, HRC)
Thomas Hall to Eliza Wilkerson, Nov. 14, 1827.
Henry Liggett, BM. (CA)
John Hankins to Elizabeth Linnett, Nov. 3, 1827.
Ebenezer Johnson, BM. (CA)
John Harvey to Abigal Cob (or Cole), Nov. 13, 1827.
William Harvey, BM. (Nov. 14, 1827) (CA, HRC)
James Hurst to Celly Sprall, May 5, 1827.
John Eblen, BM. (CA)
Cory A. James to Catherine E. Car, Aug. 8, 1827.
(HRC)
Dudley Jolly to Nelly Pierce, Jan. 3, 1827.
(Jan. 6, 1827) (CA)
Jesse K. _____ to Nancy Short, Jan. 14, 1827.
(Jan. 15, 1827) (CA)
Welding Keeling to Elizabeth Hiden, Dec. 26, 1827.
Abraham Wrinkle, BM. (CA, HRC)
Benjamine Kimbrell to Katherine Luttrell, Jan. 8, 1827.
Peterson Kim, BM. (HRC)
Alexander Lamb to Lahida Taylor, Sep. 29, 1827.
(Oct. 2, 1827) (CA)
William Lamb to Sally Wheat, Oct. 16, 1827.
Levi Wheat, BM. (CA)
Zadak Loveless to Martha Falton, Dec. 17, 1827.
William Loveless, BM. (HRC)
Obediah Mathis to Nancy Fuller, Mar. 23, 1827.
Wylie Tuton, BM. (CA)
Arthur McForland (or McFarland) to Elizabeth Sherrell,
June 5, 1827. (June 5, 1827) (CA, HRC)
Joseph J. Monger to Nancy S. Young (or Yancy), Dec. 1 (or
31), 1827. Samuel Harvey, Isaac Burris, John Cove, BM.
(CA, HRC)
Daniel (or Samuel) Oliver to Barbara Able, Jan. 17, 1827.
Livingston Branham, BM. (Jan. 17, 1827) (CA)
David Oxshare to Kaziah Rale, Mar. 29, 1827.
(CA)
Jene Paggett to Sarah Snodgrass, _____ 28, 1827.
Alexander Galbreath, BM. (CA)

ROANE COUNTY MARRIAGES

Charles W. Parks to Cealy Durham, Feb. 26, 1827.
  Richard H. Talliaferro, BM. (CA)
Jacob (or Josiah) Perry to Tampy (or Tempy) Lewellen,
  Sep. 9 (or 20), 1827. (Sep. 20, 1827) (CA, HRC)
George Pickel to Polly Mungor, Aug. 28, 1827.
  George Walker, BM. (CA)
Charles Ramkin to Elizabeth Huffman, Jan. 21, 1827.
  William Tucker, BM. (CA)
Elijah Rose (or Row) to Sinthy Jent (or Juet), Mar. 13,
  1827. Levi Bowers, BM. (Mar. 13, 1827) (CA, HRC)
William Scavitart to Leny Moore, Sep. 19, 1827.
  John Walker, BM. (CA)
William Scott to Elizabeth White, July 7, 1827.
  Luther White, BM. (CA, HRC)
Eldridge G. Sevier to Mary C. Brown, Nov. 13, 1827.
  William Dunlap, BM. (Nov. 15, 1827) (CA, HRC)
Joseph Shadrick (or Shadwick) to Susan Silvay (or Selvy),
  Aug. 21 (or 24), 1827. Willis Evans, BM. (CA, HRC)
Benjamin Suddath to Frances Norman, Dec. 28, 1827.
  William McKinney, BM. (CA)
Henry Todd to Dicy McKinney, Feb. 14, 1827.
  Thomas Gardner, BM. (CA)
Jacob Uteley to Nancy Williams, Feb. 19, 1827.
  (Feb. 23, 1827) (HRC)
Nathan Watson to Lucy Steel, Mar. 15 (or 25), 1827.
  James Parks, BM. (CA, HRC)
John Weese to Charity Dennis, Mar. 8, 1827.
  William Brannam, BM. (Mar. 12, 1827) (CA)
William Wester to Kissiah Cordwell, Dec. 4, 1827.
  Joseph Byrd, Daniel Wester, BM. (CA)
Levi (or Lear) Wheat to Katy Ditian (or Isham), Oct. 12,
  1827. James Killingsworth, Oct. 18, 1827. (CA, HRC)
Abraham Wrinkle to Susannah Brock, Dec. 26, 1827.
  Weldan Keeling, BM. (CA)

1828

Hezekiah Arms to Melisa Bond, Oct. 2, 1828.
  Daniel Clower, BM. (CA)
Wm. Beverly to Nancy Delozier, Apr. 28, 1828.
  Wm. Crow, BM. (May 24, 1828) (CA)
Alexander Black to Sarah Ann Smith, Oct. 11, 1828.
  (HRC)
Henry Breazeale to Syntha Ann McKinney, June 28, 1828.
  Robert H. Breazeale, BM. (July 3, 1828) (CA, HRC)
Jesse Carter to Betsy Sutton, _____, 1828.
  Louis Sutton, A. M. Brazeale, BM. (HRC)
Joshua Casey to Anna Haile, Sep. 10, 1828.
  Solomon Stow, BM. (HRC)
Benjamine Cates to Catherine Pendexter (or Pondexter or
  Poindexter), July 26, 1828. James Briggs, BM. (CA, HRC)
Greene Christianberry to Lucinda Jenkins, Feb. 22, 1828.
  (Feb. 28, 1828) (CA)
Featerston Clark to Rebecca Isreal, Mar. 29, 1828.
  John Goodman, BM. (CA)

47

Samuel Cox to Polly Copeland, July 17, 1828.
Lewis Burris, BM. (July 20, 1828) (CA)
John Davis to Elizabeth Loony, Oct. 25, 1828.
Preston Loony, BM. (Oct. 28, 1828) (CA)
Samuel Edmonston to Sarah Hinds, Oct. 25, 1828.
John T. East, BM. (Oct. 19, 1828) (CA)
Joseph Ellis to Synthia Nail, Apr. 10, 1828.
Allen Balton, BM. (CA)
Sylvester Freeman to Anna Ellis, Dec. 13, 1828.
William Ellis, BM. (CA)
Abraham Fuller to Katherine Collins, Jan. 3, 1828.
Samuel Jordan, BM. (CA)
William Gammon to Margart Johnson, Apr. 23, 1828.
James Killingsworth, BM. (Apr. 20, 1828) (CA)
Owing Gentry to Martha J. Brazeale, Feb. 1, 1828.
(HRC)
Henry Goddard to Sophia Fike, Feb. 20, 1828.
(July 21, 1828) (CA)
William Goddard to Nancy Evans, Nov. 5, 1828.
Nathan Goddard, BM. (HRC)
William Goodwin to Catherine Buckalow, Jan. 21, 1828.
(Jan. 24, 1828) (CA)
Annison (or Ornson) Harris to Nancy Rector, Aug. 4, 1828.
Thomas Donnahu, BM. (Aug. 6, 1828) (CA, HRC)
Albert Henderson to Elizabeth Hawks, Aug. 17, 1828.
(HRC)
Eli Hinds to Elizabeth Longacre, May 28, 1828.
Benjamine Longacre, BM. (June 10, 1828) (CA)
Albert Hurt to Sally Garrett, May 14, 1828.
(HRC)
John Jolly to Polly Deatheridge, Aug. 16 (or 19), 1828.
William Jolly, BM. (Aug. 19, 1828) (CA, HRC)
John C. Julian to Jane Taylor, Dec. 2, 1828.
Westley Sturgis, BM. (CA)
William Keeling to Anna Wringle, June 17, 1828.
Hezekiah Brock, BM. (CA)
Moses Lewis to Lucinda Shell, Dec. 20, 1828.
(HRC)
William Lovelass to Polly Minton, July 9, 1828.
Silas M. Magee, BM. (July 10, 1828) (CA, HRC)
James Magill to Betsey Cash,· July 17, 1828.
Thomas Williams, BM. (CA)
George Martin to Elizabeth McIntire, Sep. 24, 1828.
(Sep. 25, 1828) (CA, HRC)
William McCally to Polly Rather, May 28, 1828.
Waddy Thompson, BM. (HRC)
Abner McDaniel to Edney Hornsby, Aug. 27, 1828.
(CA)
Thomas McMullin to Peggy Ingram, Aug. 2, 1828.
Hugh Woody, BM. (CA)
Morris B. Mitchell to Anna Ewings, Dec. 26, 1828.
Jesse Mitchell, BM. (Jan. 8, 1829)
George Moore to Polly Waren, Apr. 2, 1828.
Samuel Alexander, BM. (CA)

ROANE COUNTY MARRIAGES

Israel Morris to Fanny Oaks, Apr. 9, 1828.
  Washington Kirkland, BM. (CA)
Barton Philpot to Catherine Funderburk, Oct. 18, 1828.
  William Pope, BM. (Oct. 19, 1828) (CA)
Littleton Pleasant to Catherine Anthony, July 23, 1828.
  Robert Stow, BM. (July 23, 1828) (CA)
James Qualls to Eliza Snow, Dec. 30, 1828.
  James Taylor, BM. (HRC)
Reynolds Ramsey to Louisa C. Lenoir, Jan. 17, 1828.
  (HRC)
John Rather to Peggy Rayburn, Feb. 28, 1828.
  William Andrew, BM. (Feb. 28, 1828) (CA)
Elijah Rector to Nancy Man, Jan. 1, 1828.
  Robert Man, BM. (CA)
Brasher Roberts to Peggy L. Rogers, Sep. 10, 1828.
  Amos Marney, BM. (CA)
Drewy Robinson to Polly Hamelton, July 31, 1828.
  Isaac Barger, BM. (Aug. 6, 1828) (CA, HRC)
Hezekiah Smith to Anna Rolston, Mar. 1 (or 10), 1828.
  Samuel Bowman, BM. (Mar. 10, 1828) (CA, HRC)
James Stephenson to Nancy Crow, Dec. 11, 1828.
  Robert Marney, BM. (Dec. 11, 1828) (CA, HRC)
Coleman Todd to Nancy Atkinson, Apr. 11, 1828.
  Henry Todd, BM. (CA)
Nicholas Ward to Margaret Queener, Mar. 18, 1828.
  George Isely, BM. (May 24, 1828) (CA)
Stephen West to Emily Selvadge, Aug. 11, 1828.
  Richard Richards, Michael Selvadge, BM. (CA)
Harvey White to Catherine Scott, Feb. 5, 1828.
  (Feb. 5, 1828) (CA)
John Wilson to Patsy Robinson, Sep. 30, 1828.
  John Purris, BM. (CA)
Thomas Woodburn to Polly Griffy, Mar. 26, 1828.
  John Campbell, BM. (Apr. 1, 1828) (CA)

1829

John Able to Betsy Evans, Apr. 2, 1829.
  (Apr. 10, 1829) (CA)
John Ayer to Jane Perine, July 2, 1829.
  (July 21, 1829) (CA)
Francis J. Baldwin to Nancy Webb, Oct. 22, 1829.
  Isaac Johnson, BM. (CA)
John Branham to Malinda Kane, Dec. 31, 1829.
  James Cooly, BM. (CA)
Evan Breeding to Abigail Hinds, Dec. 19, 1829.
  Joseph Hinds, BM. (Dec. 22, 1829) (CA, HRC)
James Brown to Martha Tolar, Apr. 10, 1829.
  George Arnold, BM. (CA)
Milton Burk to Pheby Hartley, Jan. 24, 1829.
  Lewis Rentfro, BM. (CA)
Richard Clark to Ann SMith, Jan. 26, 1829.
  James Cofer, BM. (July 25, 1829) (CA, HRC)
Abraham Copher to Frances M. Willis, Mar. 4, 1829.
  Willis Durrett, Baldwin Underwood, BM. (CA)

49

John Covington to Nancy Guffey, Jan. 3 (or 5), 1829.
 Jesse King, James Hankins, BM. (CA, HRC)
William Covington to Elizabeth Garrett, Sep. 24, 1829.
 (Sep. 24, 1829) (CA)
John Crenshaw to Amy Herbert, Dec. 14, 1829.
 John E. Nelson, BM. (Dec. 24, 1829) (CA)
John Crawford to Rebecca Woody, Sep. 15, 1829.
 (Sept. 15, 1829) (CA)
Moses Crevat to Nancy West, Jan. 15, 1829.
 Ruben West, BM. (CA)
John Davis to Jane Rayan, Jan. 27, 1829.
 Lewis Anthony, BM. (CA)
Westley Eldridge to Isabell Moore, Sep. 3, 1829.
 Walter Christian, BM. (Sep. 3, 1829) (CA)
James Ellison to Hetty Casey, Apr. 11, 1829.
 Benjamine Ragsdale, BM. (CA)
James Fell to Rebecca Tate, Mar. 24, 1829.
 Elijah Longbottom, BM. (HRC)
David Fritts to Catherine Cook, Mar. 19, 1829.
 John Cook, BM. (Sep. 19, 1829) (CA)
Thomas Fryar to Polly McNabb, Apr. 16, 1829.
 Philip Stephens, BM. (Apr. 16, 1829) (CA)
George Gallaher to Sarah Robinson, May 9, 1829.
 Wm. Galbreath, BM. (May 14, 1829) (CA)
William H. Gardner to Ann Galloway, June 30, 1829.
 Thomas Gardner, BM. (HRC)
John Gibson to Angeline Wilcocks, Oct. 24, 1829.
 James Harris, BM. (CA)
James Harris to Drusilla Gibson, May 25, 1829.
 Samuel Owings, Wm. Hall, BM. (May 28, 1829) (CA)
John Haskins to Catherine Parmer, Dec. 24, 1829.
 Allen Blair, BM. (Dec. 24, 1829) (CA)
Daniel Hicks to Viney Redman, Mar. 17, 1829.
 Wm. W. Basket, BM. (CA)
John Houston to Margaret Riddle, Feb. 20, 1829.
 Robert Stow (or Stout), BM. (Feb. 24, 1829) (CA, HRC)
William Huff to Keziah Tunnell, Sep. 24, 1829.
 James Freeman, BM. (HRC)
William Hughs to Jane Bevely, Mar. 11, 1829.
 Andrew Lilburn, BM. (CA)
Samuel Hutchison to Elizabeth Ballard, Feb. 28, 1829.
 William Ballard, BM. (CA)
Gabriel Jakewish to Levice Yandle, Apr. 6, 1829.
 Willis M. Yandle, BM. (Apr. 7, 1829) (CA)
John Jaquis to Polly Jolly, Apr. 22, 1829.
 Dudley Jolly, BM. (CA)
James Johnson to Susanna Johnson, Mar. 10, 1829.
 Samuel Johnson, BM. (CA)
John Little to Elizabeth Waren, Oct. 10, 1829.
 John Tummins, BM. (CA)
Joseph Larance to Mary Ann Hyten, Oct. 13 (or 29), 1829.
 Andrew (or Anderson) Hyten, BM. (CA, HRC)
Henry Lyle to Jenney Laney, Aug. 11, 1829.
 Henry Jenkins, BM. (Aug. 11, 1829) (CA)

ROANE COUNTY MARRIAGES

Robert Mann to Viney Richards, Feb. 21, 1829.
  George Isely, BM. (CA)
Samuel Matlock to Margaret Houston, Mar. 9, 1829.
  William Galbreath, BM. (Mar. 12, 1829) (CA)
Jesse McCloud to Malinda Walker, Aug. 5, 1829.
  Michael Henderson, William Hall, BM. (CA)
Jesse McKinney to Matilda Harvey, Feb. 23 (or 24), 1829.
  Michael Arnold, BM. (Feb. 24, 1829) (CA, HRC)
William M. Mead to Berthena Branham, May 7, 1829.
  Samuel Houston, BM. (May 7, 1829) (CA)
Noah Miller to Rachel Carter, Oct. 27, 1829.
  James Gambrill (or Gamble), BM. (HRC)
George Mitchell to Sarah Ewing, Oct. 30 (or Nov. 5), 1829.
  James W. Waren, BM. (Nov. 5, 1829) (CA, HRC)
Thomas Nesmith to Elizabeth Roberts, Jan. 29, 1829.
  Robt. S. Gilliland, BM. (CA)
James H. Norman to Nancy Wiley, Feb. 14, 1829.
  Henry H. Wiley, BM. (Feb. 26, 1829) (CA)
Joseph Overton to Polly Blevins, Dec. 7, 1829.
  William Eblen, BM. (CA)
William Owings to Abigail Randolph, Oct. 20, 1829.
  (HRC)
Samuel Parham to Crisey Givens, Jan. 8, 1829.
  Joel Hembree, BM. (Jan. 13, 1829) (CA)
Josiah Parkins to Nancy Gallaher, May 2, 1829.
  Abraham Gallaher, BM. (CA)
Lewis Parkins to Mary Hinds, Mar. 2, 1829.
  Benjamine Longacre, BM. (CA)
James Parks to Jane Carmichael, Sep. 1, 1829.
  Samuel L. Childress, BM. (Sep. __, 1829) (CA)
Noah Prewitt to Vesty Prewitt, Dec. 1, 1829.
  (CA)
John Rayburn to Lucinda Amos, Dec. 22, 1829.
  John McNutt, BM. (Dec. 24, 1829) (CA)
John Renfro to Polly Snow, Dec. 18, 1829.
  M. K. Selvidge, BM. (HRC)
Samuel Richeson to Jane Hostler, Feb. 19, 1829.
  James Bower, BM. (Feb. 19, 1829) (CA)
David Roberts to Patsey Bailey, Jan. (or June) 21, 1829.
  Isaac Bailey, BM. (CA, HRC)
Wm. Roberts to Ann Creven, July 24, 1829.
  Richard Richards, BM. (CA)
Zedekiah Roberts to Martha Barnett, Dec. 22, 1829.
  W. C. Breashears, BM. (CA)
Charles Robertson to Lois Branham, Sep. 19, 1829.
  William M. Mead, BM. (CA)
Archibald C. Rogers to Sarah P. Clark, Jan. 22, 1829.
  Robert B. Cain, BM. (CA, HRC)
Michael Selvage to Nancy Snow, Oct. 21, 1829.
  Stephen West, BM. (CA)
John Shields to Sarah Haggard, Sep. 3, 1829.
  Ruben Allen, BM. (CA)
Michael Shutterly to Malinda Powell, Jan. 26, 1829.
  (Jan. 27, 1829) (CA)

Samuel H. Smith to Teresa R. Patton, Feb. 19, 1829.
(Feb. 19, 1829) (CA)
Richard Snow to Sarah Murphy, Sep. 5, 1829.
Richard H. Talliaferro, Wm. Hall, BM. (Sep. __, 1829)
(CA)
Madison Stone to Sarah Hornsby, Oct. 26, 1829.
Alexander Grigg, BM. (CA)
Wesley Sturgess to Eliza Eblen, Dec. 16, 1829.
Thos. N. Clark, BM. (CA)
John Suddath to Eveline Center, Apr. 14, 1829.
Wm. C. McKamey, BM. (Apr. 14, 1829) (CA)
Larkin Sullins to Polly Richmond, Aug. 7, 1829.
Henry H. Wiley, BM. (Aug. 27, 1829) (CA)
John Sutton to Nancy McCall, Mar. 2, 1829.
(CA)
John Taylor to Sally Lamb, Feb. 4 (or 15), 1829.
Samuel McCarmack, BM. (Feb. 5, 1829) (CA, HRC)
James H. Underwood to Polly Russell, July 15, 1829.
Wm. Underwood, BM. (July 16, 1829) (CA)
Thomas Wallis to Jane Brook, Oct. 15, 1829.
Catherine Brook, BM. (CA)
John West to Rebecca Blanton, Feb. 11, 1829.
John Selvage, BM. (CA)
Abraham Whittenburg to Eliza Wells, Mar. 24, 1829.
Benj. Whittenburg, BM. (Mar. 24, 1829) (CA)
Isaac Wilhite (or Welhite) to Susanna Harris, Apr. 7,
1829. Orison Harris, BM. (CA, HRC)
Nathaniel Willett to Charity Russell, Sep. 24, 1829.
Thos. G. Willett, BM. (CA)
John Wilson to Malindy Marney, July 28, 1829.
James Stephenson, BM. (July 28, 1829) (CA)
John W. Winton to Eliza Browder, Aug. 19, 1829.
Henry S. Purris, BM. (Aug. 25, 1829) (CA)
Joel Wright to Amanda Westbrook, Jan. 22, 1829.
Isaac Burris, BM. (May 22, 1829) (CA)

1830

Robert Allen to Penelphia (or Penolpina) Stults, Feb. 19
(or 29), 1830. Edward Edwards, BM. (CA)
Henry Ault to Sarah P. Jones, Aug. 2, 1830.
William H. Lay, BM. (CA)
William H. Barns to Susan Roberts, Aug. 2, 1830.
Champain Westbrook, BM. (CA, HRC)
William C. Berry to Ella C. Kirk, Apr. 6, 1830.
William Galbreath, BM. (Apr. 8, 1830) (CA)
Jerimia Besher to Judy Cash, Aug. 25, 1830.
George _____, BM. (CA)
Charles Bogart to Caroline Breazeale, Sep. 15, 1830.
Abraham Bogart, BM. (CA)
Burrel Brackett to Nancy Pruiet(?), Jan. 16, 1830.
Samuel Sevier, BM. (CA)
William Brannum to Sarah Manning, Dec. 21, 1830.
Peter Manning, BM. (CA)

Joseph Breashear (or Brasheare) to Mary Dicky, Mar. 24, 1830. Thomas Gardener, BM. (Mar. 25, 1830) (CA, HRC)
William Breazeale to Elizabeth Little, Mar. 10, 1830. William P. Walker, BM. (CA)
Bryant Breeden to Sarah Longacre, Mar. 30, 1830. Benj. Longacre, Jr., BM. (Apr. 6, 1830) (CA)
Daniel Brown to Jane Ellinder, Feb. 2, 1830. Robert Noble, BM. (CA)
John Brown to Nancy Allison, Nov. 21, 1830. (Nov. 21, 1830) (CA)
Robert Brown to Nancy Allens(?), Nov. 21, 1830. Lewis W. Jordan, BM. (CA)
William B. Byrd to Elizabeth Crow, Mar. 21, 1830. Lewis Renfro, BM. (CA)
Philip Carter to Mary Ballard, Dec. 18, 1830. William Ballard, BM. (CA)
Levi Casey to Polly Haggard, Feb. 4, 1830. Alex Dugger, BM. (Feb. 4, 1830) (CA)
Pleasant Casey to Lucy Webb, July 19, 1830. Levi Casey, BM. (CA)
John I. Chaney to Hannah Selvage, Apr. 10, 1830. William Selvage, BM. (CA)
John G. Clark to Winney Jones, Oct. 8, 1830. Stephen Honey, BM. (HRC)
Jacob Clowar to Patsy Cloud, Dec. 30, 1830. James Clower, BM. (Jan. 2, 1831) (CA)
John Collier to Polly Hankins, Aug. 9, 1830. David Roberts, BM. (HRC)
James Cooly to Ann Lovelace, Aug. 19, 1830. Wm. H. Breazeale, BM. (CA)
Josiah Danforth to Letiha Prater, Dec. 8, 1830. William Prater, BM. (Dec. 9, 1830) (CA)
Alexander Davis to Sarah Liles, Dec. 20, 1830. (Dec. 24, 1830) (CA)
Floyd Dotson to Mary Renno, Nov. 11, 1830. (William Keeling) (CA)
Jonathan Doughlass to Polly Tutle, June 22, 1830. Aron Lewis, BM. (CA)
Solomon Easter to Nancy Smally, Dec. 28, 1830. Philip Small, BM. (CA)
John Eaton to Mary Ann Dawson, May 14, 1830. Silas Dawson, BM. (May 27, 1830) (CA)
John Eaton to Polly Martin, Oct. 11, 1830. Zarhariah Ayers, BM. (HRC)
William Edgman to Nancy Bishop, Feb. 22, 1830. Johnston Edgman, Joab Fouste, BM. (CA)
Samuel H. Ewing to Catherine Spence, Jan. 26, 1830. _____ Findley, BM. (Jan. 26, 1830) (CA)
Archilees Felts to Nancy Farmer, May 22, 1830. Samuel Woody, BM. (May 23, 1830) (CA)
Phillip Fritts to Frances Jane Williams, Dec. 15, 1830. Peter Fritts, BM. (HRC)
Jacob Funk to Emily Hostler (or Hastler), Nov. 30, 1830. David Patton, BM. (CA, HRC)

Alexander Getgood to Sally Bagwell, Dec. 16, 1830.
  Michael Gooden, BM. (CA)
Robert Glass to Susannah Sparks, Apr. 10, 1830.
  Richard Sparks, BM. (CA)
John Grant to Dolly Winten, Sep. 29, 1830.
  William S. Galloway, BM. (CA)
Enoch Green to Isabella Edwards, Oct. 16, 1830.
  Isaac Bullard, BM. (CA)
William Green to Milly Walker, May 6, 1830.
  Ruben Cook, BM. (CA)
Samuel Grubb to Sarah Roach, Oct. 23, 1830.
  George Pickett, BM. (Oct. __, 1830) (CA)
John D. Harbert to Elizabeth Dalton, Sep. 23, 1830.
  Rial Silvey, BM. (HRC)
Joel B. Hembree to Sally Wilhite, Jan. 26, 1830.
  (Jan. 26, 1830) (CA)
Joseph B. Hensley to Rachel Gallion, Sep. 23, 1830.
  Isaac Gallion, BM. (CA)
Henry Holder to Sophia Holder, Jan. 18, 1830.
  Linsey Tunel, BM. (Jan. 19, 1830) (CA)
John Hood to Polly Ownley, Nov. 25, 1830.
  Thos. Hood, BM. (CA)
John A. Hooke to Polly Gamble, Dec. 16, 1830.
  Milo Smith, BM. (Dec. 15, 1830) (CA)
Asa Howard to Elizabeth Prewit, Feb. 22, 1830.
  John Wiley, BM. (CA)
William Hutson to Matilda B. Wright, Sep. 10, 1830.
  Hansel Wright, BM. (HRC)
James Irwin to Rebecca McKinney, Aug. 24, 1830.
  John Crowder, BM. (Aug. 24, 1830) (CA)
J. A. James to Casander Kennedy, Mar. 5, 1830.
  William C. Julian, BM. (Mar. 6, 1830) (CA, HRC)
Ebenezer Johnson (or Johnston) to Hannah H. Huff, Aug. 2,
  1830. Robert Johnston, BM. (Aug. 5, 1830) (CA, HRC)
William Johnson to Jane Webb, Jan. 19, 1830.
  Francis Baldwin, BM. (CA)
Thomas Jones to Harritt Haggard, July 30, 1830.
  Dudley Snow, BM. (Aug. 3, 1830) (CA, HRC)
Samuel Jordan to Betsey G. Gamble, Apr. 2, 1830.
  Samuel H. Smith, BM. (CA)
Martin Keith to Elizabeth Black, Jan. 11, 1830.
  James Bowers, BM. (Jan. 11, 1830) (CA)
James Kelly to Nancy Ward, July 9, 1830.
  John Kelly, BM. (July 10, 1830) (CA)
John W. Landrum to Charity Newman, July 8, 1830.
  (July 8, 1830) (CA)
Charles Lawson to Swarthy Ann Rewett, Mar. 26, 1830.
  Henry Todd, BM. (Apr. 28, 1830) (CA)
John McCarroll to Jane Ewell, May 27, 1830.
  William W. Millican, BM. (May 27, 1830) (CA)
John McClesta to Sally Catlet, Dec. 30, 1830.
  Daniel Dunigan, BM. (CA)
John McKane to Elizabeth Dawson, Sep. 9, 1830.
  Wiley Tuten, BM. (HRC)

John McPherson to Ethelinda Mahan, Jan. 7, 1830.
John Haley, BM. (CA)
Elias Menable to Peggy Oden, Jan. 1, 1830.
Willis Stockton, BM. (CA)
John Merriott to Ruba Dunavan, July 23, 1830.
Thomas Potter, BM. (CA)
William Merritt to Elizabeth Potter, Mar. 5, 1830.
William Christenberry, BM. (Mar. 18, 1830) (CA)
Moses L. Millican to Narcissa Underwood, Nov. 20, 1830.
George W. Gains, BM. (CA)
Thomas Napier to Ethalinda Underwood, Aug. 11, 1830.
Alexander McCullough, BM. (CA)
James Oliver to Anna Stults, Dec. 23, 1830.
Westley Sturgess, BM. (CA)
George Ollis to Betsey Russell, May 11, 1830.
Thomas Asher, BM. (CA)
Jacob Parks to Susannah Bryant, Mar. 25, 1830.
Samuel Parks, BM. (Mar. 25, 1830) (CA)
Joseph Parks to Margaret Fain, Dec. 6, 1830.
Robert Blackston, BM. (HRC)
William Roberts to Lutilia Miller, Oct. 12, 1830.
William D. Miller, BM. (Oct. 12, 1830) (CA)
Shirley Russell to Sally Berry, Aug. 15, 1830.
William Russell, Henry Davidson, BM. (Aug. 15, 1830.
(CA)
William Sellers to Margaret Matheny, Jan. 16, 1830.
Elijah Matheny, BM. (Jan. 21, 1830) (CA)
John Smith to Julian Davis, Mar. 8, 1830.
William Ellis, BM. (Mar. 25, 1830) (CA)
John Y. Smith to Leah A. Lenoir, Feb. 17, 1830.
Thomas N. Clark, BM. (Feb. 19, 1830) (CA)
William Smith to Nancy Miller, Mar. 9, 1830.
William Holland, BM. (CA)
John Spralt to Nancy Thompson, Dec. 8, 1830.
James Owen, BM. (CA)
Jefferson Stormen to Vanilia Patty, Dec. 25, 1830.
Adam Tenor, BM. (CA)
Benjamine Tanner to Mary McPherson, July 24, 1830.
John East, BM. (CA)
Alfred Thompson to Julia Woody, Nov. 20, 1830.
Brice Woody, BM. (HRC)
Robert B. Tucker to Sarah Newman, July 15, 1830.
John A. Hooke, BM. (July 15, 1830) (CA)
Samuel Tunnel to Sarah C. McKinney, Mar. 22, 1830.
Wm. C. McKinney, BM. (CA)
David Turpin to Dillid Wiatte, Mar. 23, 1830.
Thos. Turpin, BM. (CA)
Absolum Tuten to Nancy Bracket, Mar. 4, 1830.
William Ballard, BM. (CA)
Thomas Walker to Polly James, Jan. 1, 1830.
Wm. H. Gardner, BM. (Jan. 7, 1830) (CA)
Martin Watson to Catherine Jones, Nov. 23, 1830.
John Nail, BM. (CA)
William S. Weese to Nancy Weese, Jan. 28, 1830.
William Weese, BM. (HRC)

Green West to Polly Davis, Aug. 9, 1830.
Reuben West, BM. (Aug. 9, 1830) (CA)
Thomas Williams to Mahala Gammon, Oct. 2, 1830.
William Davis, BM. (Oct. 12, 1830) (CA)
William Williams to Mary Hicks, Dec. 28, 1830.
Philip Fritts, BM. (CA)
James Wilmot to Maria Ayer (or Burnett), Mar. 31, 1830.
Zacheus Wyer, Alen Sutherland, BM. (Apr. 2, 1830)
(CA, HRC)
Abraham Woody to Ann Vaughn, Aug. 21, 1830.
Charles Bogart, BM. (CA)

1831

James Alexander to Elmira Warren, Jan. 25, 1831.
John Spence, BM. (CA)
Jonathan Bagwell to Polly Brown, Sep. 24, 1831.
William Lams, BM. (CA)
Edward Bowman to Sally Cooper, June 22, 1831.
Jesse M. Low, BM. (HRC)
William Branham to Rebecca Lyles, Apr. 14, 1831.
William Brock, BM. (HRC)
Jediah W. Breazeale to Judiah Lay, May 23, 1831.
David Breazeale, BM. (CA)
Pleasant M. Breazeale to Jane McMullin, Oct. 10, 1821.
Philip Beddo, BM. (CA)
Edward H. Brown to Charlott Taylor, Aug. 5, 1831.
John Cooly, BM. (CA)
William Brown to Lititia Kindred, May 29, 1831.
(HRC)
John H. Bryant to Sarah Ann Hunt, Oct. 5, 1831.
John Black, BM. (CA)
David Burnett to Patsy Burnett, Feb. 18 (or 20), 1831.
Innis _____, BM. (Feb. 20, 1831) (CA)
William Carroll to Betsey Tindel, June 22, 1831.
Metiweather Smith, BM. (CA)
Moses L. Carter to Synthea McCarroll, Oct. 25, 1831.
(Oct. 26, 1831) (CA)
James Cosby to Elosia Hotchkiss, Feb. 4, 1831.
Mathew Shelton, BM. (CA)
John Cox to Ann (or Ana) Crow, Jan. 14 (or 15), 1831.
Peter Manning, BM. (Jan. 15, 1831) (CA, HRC)
Nathaniel L. Davis to Malinda Oden, June 13, 1831.
John Oden, BM. (CA)
David Dearmond to Sarah Hinds, Oct. 5, 1831.
Zacheus Ayers, BM. (HRC)
James Deatherage to Elizabeth Ahart, May 13, 1831.
James Matheny, BM. (CA)
George Delozier to Sally Stewart, July 8, 1831.
John McDaniel BM. (CA)
Richerson Earp to Sarah Tolbert, July 11, 1831.
Henry Liggett, BM. (CA)
John Eaton (or Easton) to Polly Martin (or Clark),
Oct. 11, 1831. Zacheus Ayer, BM. (Oct. 11, 1831) (CA,
HRC)

Edward Edwards to Charletta Toatum, Dec. 26, 1831.
   John B. Mason, BM. (CA)
Calib Ellis to Hannah Hankins, July 16, 1831.
   Joseph Byrd, BM. (CA)
Charles Ellis to Vicey Turner, Mar. 12, 1831.
   Archilla L. Harrison, BM. (HRC)
William Ellis to Anna W. Waller, Dec. 17, 1831.
   Philip Bedo, BM. (CA)
Thomas England to Nancy Dugger, Dec. 28, 1831.
   Thomas Lowe, BM. (Dec. 29, 1831) (CA)
Samuel P. Forrester to Abegail Yoakley, Aug. 31, 1831.
   Wm. Lovelace, BM. (CA)
Henry Fritts to Mary Williams, July 2, 1831.
   Peter Fritts, BM. (CA)
Abraham Fuller to Nancy Scott, June 19, 1831.
   John McCormick, Jefferson Burnett, BM. (CA)
Essau Funk to Dicey Hostler, Oct. 4, 1831.
   Austin Green, BM. (CA)
Archibald Gilbert to Sally Allen, May 19, 1831.
   Thomas Heath, BM. (May 19, 1831) (CA)
Isaac Griffith to Catherine Howard, June 6, 1831.
   Josiah Sullens, BM. (HRC)
Moses Grigg to Nancy Padgett, Aug. 18, 1831.
   George Ayhart, BM. (CA)
Lutherate Grigsby to Patsey Bailey, Oct. 8, 1831.
   George Good, BM. (HRC)
Hiram Grunnit to Patsy Yoakum, Sep. 19, 1831.
   Wm. Reynolds, BM. (CA)
James Hackney to _____ Londean (or Longacre), Sep. 12,
   1831. D. Parkings, BM. (HRC)
James Harrison to Sarah Merrick, Aug. 3, 1831.
   John Dyke, BM. (CA)
Elijah Harwood to Sarah Loiner, Dec. 26, 1831.
   Wm. McKamey, BM. (Dec. 26, 1831) (CA)
Hardy Holems to Sarah White, Nov. 12, 1831.
   Allen White, BM. (Nov. 13, 1831) (CA)
Lemastin V. (or Lemaster) Hornsby to Polly Donaldson,
   Feb. 14 (or 15), 1831. Benjamin Longacre, BM. (Feb. 15,
   1831) (CA, HRC)
Thomas Ives to Polly McNite, Jan. __, 1831.
   John E. Nelson, BM. (CA)
John Jinkins to Sally Rayburn, Sep. 22, 1831.
   William Snow, BM. (Sep. 29, 1831) (CA)
James Johnson to Martha M. Johnson, May 5, 1831.
   Robert Johnson, BM. (May 10, 1831) (CA)
John Langly to Lanca Proctor, June 14, 1831.
   Robert Powers, BM. (CA)
Isaac L. Low to Malinda Matlock, Mar. 31, 1831.
   William Galbreath, BM. (CA)
William Magill to Francis M. Evans, Mar. 14, 1831.
   Wm. C. McKamey, BM. (CA)
James Martin to Evaline Gossett, Mar. 20, 1831.
   John Wm. Breazeale, BM. (Mar. 20, 1831) (CA)
James Martin to Polly Young, June 18, 1831.
   George Martin, BM. (CA)

William L. McEwen to Matilda V. Clark, Dec. 15, 1831.
Isaac T. Lenoir, BM. (Dec. 15, 1831) (CA)
James Melton to Eliza Foster, Oct. 10, 1831.
Alexander Nail, BM. (HRC)
Jacob Messamore to Lettice Tunnel, Oct. 3, 1831.
William I. Huff, BM. (Oct. 5, 1831) (CA, HRC)
Joseph Overton to Peggy Morris, Sep. 22, 1831.
Linsey Tunnell, BM. (CA)
Samuel Parrine to Edith E. Longacre, Nov. 13, 1831.
Bryant Breeding, BM. (CA)
Uriah A. Preston to Abigail Parmley, Aug. 27, 1831.
James Preston, BM. (CA)
Henry L. Purris to Esther A. Clowney, Oct. 6, 1831.
William M. McEwen, BM. (Oct. 6, 1831) (CA)
Landon Rector to Betsey Taliferro, Jan. 24 (or 25), 1831.
William Steen, BM. (Jan. 25, 1831) (CA, HRC)
Armstead Redman to Elvira Hughs, July 22, 1831.
Abraham Hughs, BM. (CA)
Mark Rentfroe to Hepsiby Burk, Jan. 29, 1831.
Patrick Evans, BM. (CA)
George Reynolds to Sarah Taylor, May 11, 1831.
Wyley Tuten, BM. (CA)
John Roberson to Elizabeth Sylar, Mar. 30, 1831.
Samuel Wright, BM. (CA)
Solomon Row to Martha Coleman, June 11, 1831.
Burris Short, BM. (CA)
George Scarborough to Esther Christenberry, Jan. 29, 1831.
Moses White, BM. (Jan. 31, 1831) (CA)
Rial Silvey to Celia Johnston, Nov. 3, 1831.
Valentine Cunningham, BM. (Nov. 3, 1831) (CA)
Isaac Smith to Flora McMillan, Sep. 14, 1831.
Thomas Branham, BM. (CA, HRC)
John Y. Smith to Leah Lenoir, Feb. 19, 1831.
Thomas N. Clark, BM. (HRC)
Lewis M. Sumpter to Lidia Geren, Jan. 31, 1831.
John Smith(or Smithy), BM. (Feb. 1, 1831) (CA, HRC)
Drewy Thompson to Levina Hutson, Oct. 1, 1831.
Andrew Miles, BM. (CA)
Robert Thornton to Sarah Hagler, Nov. 1, 1831.
John Hagler, BM. (CA)
Denny Turner to Elizabeth Cardwell, May 28, 1831.
John S. Shields, BM. (CA)
David M. Wade to Elizabeth Brumley, Sep. 30, 1831.
Lewis Kirkpatrick, BM. (CA)
William F. Walker to Martha Stockton, Aug. 27, 1831.
Ruben Allen, BM. (CA)
Leander Watson to Mary Ann Stubbs (or Suttle), Oct. 24,
1831. Richard Cox, BM. (CA, HRC)
Joseph Williams to Julie Ann Lower, Sep. 20, 1831.
Michael Lower, BM. (CA)
James Yandell to Polly Woolsey (or Williams), June 4, 1831.
Dudley Jolly, Solomon Row, BM. (CA, HRC)

Francis Adams to Famellia Green, Dec. 5, 1832.
Churchwell Jackson, BM. (CA)
Joshiah I. Bacon to Mary Toliver, Jan. 17, 1832.
Josiah Jackson, BM. (CA)
Lowery A. Bacon to Matilda Stone, Oct. 11, 1832.
Washington Ballard, BM. (CA)
Haram Booker to Sarah Nicholson, Dec. 19, 1832.
(Dec. 19, 1832) (CA)
John Brandon to Elizabeth Henson, Dec. 20, 1832.
Jonathan Henson, BM. (CA)
John Campbell to Pheby Booth, Oct. 20, 1832.
Girvel Good, BM. (CA)
John Copeland to Ann Suel, June 12, 1832.
James Seal, BM. (CA)
Alexander Davis to Sarah Liles, Dec. 20, 1832.
Henry Ligget, BM. (CA)
George Davis to Mary Ann Watson, Nov. 19, 1832.
William Waller, BM. (CA)
John Dyke to Sarah Houston, Jan. 4, 1832.
Archibald Rhea, BM. (CA)
James Francis to William Ellis(?) Sep. 7, 1832.
(CA)
James Madison Freeman to Lucinda Simmons, Oct. 17, 1832.
(CA)
Josiah Gent to Jane Noel, Oct. 27, 1832.
Jacob Sullins, BM. (CA)
William Gilbert to Elizabeth Hart, Mar. 30, 1832.
James James, BM. (Apr. 1, 1832) (CA)
David Grammer to Hannah Booths, Aug. 14, 1832.
(CA)
Washington Grammer to Ruth Boothe, Apr. 3, 1832.
Aron Boothe, BM. Apr. 3, 1832. (CA)
Robert Hester to Eliza Todd, Nov. 8, 1832.
James Richardson, BM. (Nov. 8, 1832) (CA)
James F. Hicks to Angelina Boyd, Dec. 4, 1832.
John Cunningham, BM. (Dec. 4, 1832) (CA)
William Hostler to Louisa Nichols, Oct. 8, 1832.
Lewis Kirkpatrick, BM. (CA)
Martin Howard to Nisy Cook, Oct. 18, 1832.
Rial Silvey, BM. (CA)
Nathaniel Johnson to Polly Little, Jan. 31, 1832.
John Cook, BM. (Jan. 31, 1832) (CA)
John Kade to Louisa Deatherage, Sep. 26, 1832.
Josiah Kindred to Abigail Parmer, Mar. 5, 1832.
Jesse Low, BM. (CA)
John Kinkade to _____ Kennell, Oct. 15, 1832.
Biven Kennell, BM. (CA)
Samuel Lane to Fanny Robinson, Jan. 12, 1832.
(Jan. 17, 1832) (CA)
Pleasant M. Lea to Martha H. Craven, Feb. 13, 1832.
(Feb. 16, 1832) (CA)
David Little to Charity Ross, Dec. 3, 1832.
John Martin, BM. (Dec. 5, 1832) (CA)
Edw. Luttrell to Rachel Booth, July 30, 1832.
(July 30, 1832) (CA)

Martin Luttrell to Elizabeth Goforth, Dec. 29, 1832.
Robert Tucker, BM. (CA)
Robert Magill to Perlitha Bundum, Nov. 16, 1832.
Wm. Goodman, BM. (CA)
Tolbut McCall to Petina England, July 29, 1832.
Jesse M. Lowe, BM. (July 29, 1832) (CA)
John McEwin to Nancy M. Patton, Dec. 11, 1832.
(Dec. 11, 1832) (CA)
James McIntire to Mahala Tunnell, Apr. 21, 1832.
D. Mansfield, BM. (May 1, 1832) (CA)
Peter McKane to Polly Brock, May 5, 1832.
(May 6, 1832) (CA)
Andrew McNabb to Francis Christian, Aug. 28, 1832.
(Aug. 28, 1832) (CA)
Peter Monger to Elizabeth Snow, July 30, 1832.
(July 31, 1832) (CA)
James P. Montgomery to Martha Montgomery Clowney (no
date given). Henry S. Purris, BM. (Apr. 24, 1832) (CA)
Robert Morris to Peggy Finly, Aug. 7, 1832.
Daniel Wester, Joseph Brittain, BM. (CA)
Thomas Osburn to Mary Jane Wiggins, Oct. 15, 1832.
Wm. H. Wright, BM. (Oct. 17, 1832) (CA)
Philip Patterson to Mahala James, Dec. 9, 1832.
Caleb Gibson, BM. (Dec. 9, 1832) (CA)
Smith Phillips to Fanny Cofer, Dec. 19, 1832.
Absolom Adkisson, BM. (CA)
Oliver Powell to Sally Adams, Mar. 6, 1832.
Wm. Mitchell, BM. (Mar. 6, 1832) (CA)
William Ramsey to Betsey Moore, Mar. 20, 1832.
John C. McEwin, BM. (Mar. 20, 1832) (CA)
Jesse Rayburn to Barbara Tallant, July 11, 1832.
(July 19, 1832) (CA)
William Rector to Elizabeth Matheny, Dec. 12, 1832.
T. L. Ferguson, BM. (CA)
Isaac Roberts to Elizabeth Lyle, Feb. 28, 1832.
David Lyles, BM. (Feb. 28, 1832) (CA)
Samuel Roberts to Polly Jinkins, Jan. 9, 1832.
(CA)
William Robison to Dalinda Thompson, Dec. 9, 1832.
Caleb Gibson, BM. (Dec. 9, 1832) (CA)
Isiah Sellers to Nancy Todd, Oct. 22, 1832.
(Oct. 24, 1832) (CA)
Martin Silvey to Prudy Merritt, Aug. 9, 1832.
Rial Silvey, BM. (Aug. 9, 1832) (CA)
Fielding Snow to Mary Pickel, Aug. 29, 1832.
(Aug. 30, 1832) (CA)
John Spence to Mary Finly, Dec. 12, 1832.
Pleasant Ponder, BM. (CA)
Rufus Stephens to Nancy King, Oct. 11, 1832.
Wm. S. Mason, BM. (Oct. 16, 1832) (CA)
Thomas Stockton to Letitia Young, Nov. 19, 1832.
John Shell, BM. (Nov. 22, 1832) (CA)
Smith Stogdon to Martha Oaks, Jan. 20, 1832.
John Wilson, BM. (CA)

ROANE COUNTY MARRIAGES

Francis Suddath to Elizabeth Normal, Dec. 7, 1832.
  George Arnold, BM. (CA)
Isaac Tate to Sarah Capps, Oct. 24, 1832.
  George Fuller, BM. (CA)
Umphrey Thacker to Judah Williams, Jan. 2, 1832.
  George Arnold, BM. (CA)
Gilbert Wear to Angeline Strain, Dec. 17, 1832.
  Henry Liggett, BM. (CA)
Abraham Wesse to Mary Kate McIntire, Dec. 24, 1832.
  Archibald McIntire, BM. (CA)
Bloomer White to Penelope Stubbs, Apr. 4, 1832.
  James Aikens, BM. (CA)
John White to Elizabeth Able, Oct. 8, 1832.
  Joseph Able, BM. (CA)
James Willett to Christine Campbell, Aug. 9, 1832.
  Anthony H. Dicky, BM. (CA)
Andrew J. Willis to Elizabeth Asher, Mar. 24, 1832.
  (CA)
Brice Woody to Elizabeth Bogart, Mar. 31, 1832.
  Hugh Woody, BM. (CA)

1833

Joseph Able to Sarah Wilcox, Jan. 5, 1833 (or 1832).
  Wm. Smith, BM. (CA)
Drewy A. Bacon to Caroline Ballard, July 20, 1833.
  A. P. Vaughn, BM. (CA)
Pleasant Bailey to Jenetta Matheny, Sep. 17, 1833.
  (CA)
David Ball to Dravy Davis, Dec. 21, 1833.
  Wm. Breeden, BM. (CA)
Willaim Boyd to Nancy Small, Feb. 7, 1833 (or 1832).
  Jesse Redman, BM. (CA)
Malakiah Branham to Betsey Delaney, June 7, 1833.
  John Owins, BM. (CA)
Noah Branham to Peggy Watt, Apr. 23, 1833.
  Barnett Don, BM. (CA)
John Breeden to Lurana Yoakley, Feb. 23, 1833.
  (Feb. 24, 1833) (CA)
Samuel Childress to Ann Berry, Jan. 7, 1833.
  Henry Wiley, BM. (Jan. 7, 1833) (CA)
James Click to Alla Vandegrift, Sep. 14, 1833.
  Pleasant H. Lephew, BM. (Sep. 22, 1833) (CA)
William Gwin to Charity McCowan, Aug. 14, 1833.
  (Aug. 15, 1833) (CA)
Joel Hacker to Sarah Clark, Apr. 1, 1833.
  James Wakefield, John Walker, BM. (CA)
John Haley to Eliza Cravens, May 20, 1833.
  Wm. McPherson, BM. (May 24, 1833) (CA)
Gillington Hart to Elizabeth Heath, Dec. 11, 1833.
  Brice Woody, BM. (CA)
Abraham Haust(?) to Malinda Jolly, Mar. 12, 1833.
  (Mar. 12, 1833) (CA)
William Henley to Margaret E. Suddath, Nov. 11, 1833.
  Richard S. Suddath, BM. (CA)

61

Joseph Higgins to Nancy Tindell, Sep. 26, 1833.
   Calvin Newport, BM. (Oct. 3, 1833) (CA)
John W. Hill to Maria Winton, Jan. 26, 1833.
   Wyley B. Winton, BM. (CA)
Joab Johnson to Rhoda Amos, Sep. 13, 1833.
   (CA)
Robert Johnson to Francis Ewing, Jan. 1, 1833.
   Morris Mitchell, BM. (CA)
Mathis Kelly to Malinda Vaughn, Feb. 6, 1833.
   James Kelly, BM. (CA)
Josiah Kindrid to Abigail Parmer, Mar. 5, 1833.
   (Mar. 5, 1833) (CA)
Wm. Lacy to Keziah Grimley (or Grinsley), Dec. 24, 1833.
   Wm. Sewell, BM. (Dec. 26, 1833) (CA, HRC)
Hiram Lane to Sarah Snow, Mar. 30, 1833.
   (CA)
Thomas Lane to Mary Jane Hayse, Oct. 17, 1833.
   Thomas R. Lane, BM. (CA)
Allen Letsinger to Elizabeth Cole, July 24, 1833.
   License issed in Knox County, TN. (July 25, 1833) (HRC)
John J. London to Judiah Burnett, Feb. 27, 1833.
   (May 2, <u>1836</u>) (CA)
L. Addison Lyle to Esther Alexander, Feb. 7, 1833.
   Wm. Galbraith, BM. (CA)
John Magill to Polly Vaughn, Nov. 6, 1833.
   Robert Magill, BM. (CA)
George Matene to Polly West, Apr. 23, 1833.
   William West, BM. (CA)
Jacob McDaniel to Matilda Robinson, May 10, 1833.
   Martin Powell, BM. (CA)
David McLure to Louise Mitchell, July 20, 1833.
   John McLure, BM. (CA)
Hugh L. W. McPherson to Francis Ballard, Mar. 6, 1833.
   (CA)
Wm. O. Mead to Polly B. Luttrell, Nov. 21, 1833.
   (CA)
C. L. Murrey to Amanda Jones, June 23, 1833.
   Wm. Galbreath, BM. (June 23, 1833) (CA)
Elijah Perkins to Elizabeth Winton, Oct. 29, 1833.
   Rufus M. Stevins, BM. (CA)
Turner Phillips to Lorenda Allen, Dec. 16, 1833.
   Smith Philips, BM. (Dec. 17, 1833) (CA)
Pleasant Ponder to Sarah Bogart, Sep. 2, 1833.
   James Freeman, BM. (CA)
Robert Powell to Elizabeth Luttrell, Apr. 22, 1833.
   Samuel Childress, BM. (CA)
Samuel Puryear to Susan O. Hudson, Feb. 7, 1833.
   Overton P. Goodwin, BM. (Feb. 7, 1833) (CA)
James C. Queener to Mary K. Boxer, Feb. 8, 1833.
   George Isely, BM. (CA)
Charles W. Rice to Eliza Haley, Mar. 20, 1833.
   John C. Haley, BM. (Mar. 20, 1833) (CA)
Adam Rooker to Sarah Nicholson, Dec. 19, 1833.
   Abel Jackson, BM. (CA)

James Stone to Mariline Browder, Mar. 11, 1833.
(May 2, 1833) (CA)
Claibourn Stubbs to Mary E. Jones, Aug. 29, 1833.
James G. Eblen, BM. (CA)
Kinchen Tally to Mary Hulsey, Feb. 26, 1833.
(Feb. 22, 1833) (CA)
Dennis Taylor to Elizabeth Webb, May 2, 1833.
Malcomb Johnston, BM. (CA)
Stephen Townsley to Martha Breazeale, Mar. 17, 1833.
Pleasant Ponder, BM. (CA)
Sterling Turner to Esther Erwin, Dec. 24, 1833.
Wm. Wright, BM. (CA)
William Waller to Mary M. Syler, June 17, 1833.
George Davis, BM. (CA)
Martin Webb to Litha Davis, Sep. 23, 1833.
Charles Davis, BM. (CA)
John West to Sarah Rentfro, Sep. 2, 1833.
John I, Channy, BM. (CA)
William Whalan to Polly Brittan, May 18, 1833.
Jacob Waren, BM. (CA)
Elisha Williamson to Rebecca Man, Oct. 26, 1833.
James H. Miller, BM. (CA)
John Wintin to Fanny Mitchell, Apr. 27, 1833.
Wiley B. Winton, BM. (May 2, 1833) (CA)
William Wyatt to Martha Deatherage, Oct. 6, 1833.
Eldridge Oden, BM. (CA)
H. K. Yoakum to Eveline Cannon, Feb. 10, 1833.
E. D. Murray, BM. (Feb. 13, 1833) (CA)

1834

Nelson A. Adams to Patsey Mathis, June 22, 1834.
Kinchen Matthis, BM. (CA)
Terry Adkisson to Fanny Maberry, Sep. 25, 1834.
(Sep. 30, 1834) (CA)
Stephen Barksdale to William Ellis(?), July 1, 1834.
(CA)
Larkin H. Blake to Rachel Mitchell, Sep. 8, 1834.
William Blake, BM. (CA)
Wm. Blevins to Betsey Dupee, May 8, 1834.
John Doughty, BM. (CA)
John Brackett to Permelia Brackett, Oct. 1, 1834.
(CA)
John Brandon to Mary Ann Holland, Nov. 19, 1834.
Joshua Moore, BM. (CA)
Thomas Brown to Jane M. Patton, Apr. 10, 1834.
Henry H. Wiley, BM. (CA)
Carson Capps to Rebecca King, June 11, 1834.
Wm. King, BM. (CA)
Alfred Carroll to Bisher Miller, June 27, 1834.
Samuel L. Childress, BM. (CA)
Jacob Cawood to Nancy Dehart, Aug. 2, 1834.
(Aug. 14, 1834) (CA)
Walter Christian to Jan Helms, Oct. 11, 1834.
Hugh Blair, BM. (CA)

Claibourn Chumley to Mary Johnson, July 21, 1834.
 Isaac Burris, BM. (CA)
William Clift to Mary Penlan, Mar. 4, 1834.
 William McChaney, BM. (Mar. 24, 1834) (CA)
Thomas Cofer to Sarah Wake, Apr. 30, 1834.
 Noah Fisher, BM. (CA)
James Crew to Anna Lawson, July 17, 1834.
 Henton Lawson, BM. (July 18, 1834) (CA)
Owen Davis to Nancy Mann, Oct. 3, 1834.
 William Husong, BM. (Oct. 5, 1834) (CA)
Silas Dawson to Polly Varner, Jan. 2 (or 20), 1834.
 David Varner, BM. (CA)
Gideon Dennis to Jane Patty, Apr. 22, 1834.
 John Brown, BM. (CA)
Wm. Don to Comfort Wilhite, Aug. 5, 1834.
 Jesse Copeland, BM. (CA)
Charles Ellis to Vicey Turner, Mar. 12, 1834.
 Archillas Hanison, BM. (CA)
Willis Evans to Rebecca Shaddrick, Nov. 8, 1834.
 William Kane, BM. (CA)
William L. Foute to Mary Williams, Feb. 17, 1834.
 (Feb. 17, 1834) (CA)
Littleton Freeman to Sarah McMullin, Dec. 15, 1834.
 John Turner, BM. (CA)
Benjamine Gilbert to Malinda James, Nov. 22, 1834.
 Geo. W. Smith, BM. (Nov. 22, 1834) (CA, HRC)
Wm. Goens to Ann Baker, May 13, 1834.
 Joseph Brittain, BM. (CA)
Nathaniel Haggard to Jane Leonard, Nov. 17, 1834.
 (Dec. 19, 1834) (CA)
Robert Hail to Polly Rhea, Mar. 20, 1834.
 (Mar. 20, 1834) (CA) '
John Hamelton to Rachel P. Wester, Feb. 13, 1834.
 Daniel Wester, BM. (CA)
Elijah Heath to Malinda Littleton, Dec. 27, 1834.
 William H. Breazeale, BM. (CA)
Abner Hester to May Breashears, July 8, 1834.
 Edward Dickey, BM. (CA)
Vincent Jones to Charlotte Ghent, Nov. 18, 1834.
 Chas. L. Clark, BM. (CA)
Charles Magill to Nancy D. Evans, Aug. 4, 1834.
 Josiah Montgomery, BM. (CA)
John Mahaffee to Malinda Branham, Dec. 23, 1834.
 Joshua Moore, BM. (HRC)
William Majors to Prudence Rhea, May 11, 1834.
 William Underwood, BM. (CA)
Lindsy Mathis to Susannah Howell, June 2, 1834.
 Benjamine Howell, BM. (CA)
Wm. Mathis to Sarah Littleton, Mar. 21, 1834.
 John Williamson, BM. (CA)
Andrew McCullough to Elvira Underwood, Dec. 20, 1834.
 Philip Beddo, BM. (Dec. 21, 1834) (CA, HRC)
John McIntire to Nancy Martin, Aug. 30, 1834.
 George Stewart, BM. (CA)

Thomas McLain to Eliza Yandell, Aug. 6, 1834.
James Yandle, BM. (CA)
Samuel Mead to Elizabeth Hudson, Mar. 30, 1834.
Robt. W. Hudson, BM. (CA)
Richard Moorehead to Volly Berry, Aug. 15, 1834.
Wm. McChaney, BM. (CA)
James Morgan to Sarah Burk, Apr. 15, 1834.
Joseph Moss, BM. (CA)
John Morgan to May Ann Highton, Oct. 30, 1834.
Jesse Baldwin, BM. (Oct. 31, 1834) (CA, HRC)
Uriah Phillips to Loretta Jane Allen, Dec. 24, 1834.
George W. Yost, BM. (Dec. 25, 1834) (CA)
Wiley Richmond to Mahala Hassler, Sep. 25, 1834.
Wm. Hassler, BM. (CA)
Mathew D. Russell to Charlotte Dunwold, Nov. 5, 1834.
Bryson Hood, BM. (HRC)
William Russell to Judy Johnson, Aug. 19, 1834.
(Aug. 25, 1834) (CA)
Zachariah Shackleford to Mary Ann Cox, Oct. 15, 1834.
John W. Darnell, BM. (CA)
Benjamine Snow to Martha Deatherage, July 7, 1834.
George Ahart, BM. (CA)
William Soward to Mary Manning, _____, 1834(?).
Peter Manning, BM. (CA)
Richard Stegall to Elizabeth Roberts, Dec. 2, 1834.
William Roberts, BM. (CA)
Joseph Stukesberry to Nancy Rutherford, Mar. 29, 1834.
(May 2, 1834) (CA)
William A. Thompson to Elizabeth Gibbons, Nov. 26, 1834.
Ralph Smith, BM. (HRC)
Sam'l. Weese to Rebecca Weese, Feb. 26, 1834.
William Reese, BM. (CA)
Claiborn Wilkerson to Lucy Ann Pearson, May 21, 1834.
John Pearson, BM. (May 26, 1834) (no reference)
Roger Wilkey to Mariah West, Oct. 29, 1834.
Nimrod Newman, BM. (CA)
James Williamson to Nancy Woody, July 21, 1834.
(July 29, 1834) (CA)
Amos Wilson to Betsey Mullins, Oct. 3, 1834.
George Arnold, BM. (CA)

1835

John Alford to Sarah Maddy, Mar. 9, 1835.
(HRC)
David N. Bell to Eliza Ann Marley, June 19, 1835.
Jacob H. Brown, BM. (CA)
Massey Bishop to Mary W. Gideon, Aug. 5, 1835.
(May 2, 1835) (CA, HRC)
Hugh Blackwell to Huldah Barnett, Aug. 11, 1835.
Edward Dickey, BM. (CA)
Thomas G. Blythe to Permelia Cooley, May 12, 1835.
James M. Montgomery, BM. (CA)
Linsey Branham to Betsey Cooley, May 6, 1835.
Westley Middleton, BM. (May 7, 1835) (CA)

John Burnett to Olly Neil(?), Oct. 27, 1835) (CA)
  (CA)
Laird Burns to Ann Mann, Jan. 1, 1835.
  James Burns, BM. (Jan. 1, 1835) (CA)
James Campbell to Dolly Brunetta Burnett, Jan. 28, 1835.
  (Jan. 29, 1835) (CA)
Hiram Carroll to Sarah Perry, Jan. 9, 1835.
  Wm. Goodman, BM. (CA)
Wilson Carson to Jemima Burnett, July 18, 1835.
  Harmon McCastand, BM. (CA)
James Carter to Nancy Capps, Oct. 27, 1835.
  Landon Weese, BM. (Oct. 29, 1835) (CA)
Joseph Carter to Locky Luttrell, Nov. 30, 1835.
  Moses L. Carter, BM. (CA)
George Chambers to Mary Vaughn, Mar. 14, 1835.
  N. McEwin, BM. (CA)
John H. Cook to Elizabeth Liles, Mar. 6, 1835.
  Wiley Barnett, BM. (CA)
James Crow to Jane Rector, Dec. 8, 1835.
  Harris Pryor, BM. (Dec. 11, 1835) (CA)
Andrew Davis to Sally Russell, Mar. 6, 1835.
  Robert Lyle, BM. (CA)
Nathan Davis to Polly Don, May 30, 1835.
  Barnett Don, BM. (CA)
Samuel Davis to Elizabeth C. Evans, Aug. 8, 1835.
  Brice Woody, BM. (May 2, 1835) (CA)
John Day to Sarah Crowder, Sep. 15, 1835.
  Geo. Gillispie, BM. (CA)
Samuel Day to Sally West, Oct. 3, 1835.
  Henry Fleener, BM. (CA)
Samuel J. Dearmond to Grizzy B. Dearmond, Nov. 18, 1835.
  John Dearmond, BM. (CA)
Jacob Delmon to Margaret Keelough, Oct. 5, 1835.
  William H. Burris, BM. (Oct. 5, 1835) (CA)
Major M. Dobbins to Eveline F. Miller, Apr. 7, 1835.
  Ephraim Miller, BM. (Apr. 7, 1836(?) (CA)
Mathew Duff to Susan West, Mar. 21, 1835.
  John West, BM. (CA)
John Dugger to Patsy Crow, Mar. 3, 1835.
  Rufus Keith, BM. (CA)
John Ellis to Sarah Jane Margrave, Sep. 28, 1835.
  Philip Beddo, BM. (CA)
John Finley to Gabriella M. Hotchkiss, Aug. 13, 1835.
  Samuel Hotchkiss, BM. (HRC)
John Wood Francis to Nancy McKinny, Dec. 31, 1835.
  David Hood, BM. (CA)
Henry Fritts to Patsey Lyle, Mar. 6, 1835.
  John Lile, BM. (CA)
James Gibson to Mary A. Able, Dec. 12, 1835.
  David Able, BM. (CA)
William Giles to Margaret Hensley, Sep. 14, 1835.
  James Gamble, BM. (CA)
Overton Goodwin to Elizabeth Hotchkiss, June 9, 1835.
  Bryson Hood, BM. (CA)

Joshua Gordon to Polly Grammer, July 27, 1835.
(HRC)
William M. Grubb to Prudence Scarbrough, Jan. 17, 1835.
John Edwards, BM. (Jan. 20, 1835) (CA, HRC)
Allen Harp to Peggy Graham, Sep. 19, 1835.
Robert Love, BM. (CA)
Bryson Hood to Polly Ann Rector, Aug. 17, 1835.
Robert Duncan, BM. (CA)
Albert Howard to Levinia Bowling, Feb. 11, 1835.
John W. Rhea, BM. (HRC)
Ephraim Huffine to Hanover Ingram, Oct. 20 (or 30), 1835.
Thomas Melvin, BM. (Oct. 20, 1835) (CA, HRC)
Thomas Ives to Mary Silvey, Oct. 8, 1835.
Thomas Silvey, BM. (CA)
Levi Jackson to Jane West, Nov. 26, 1835.
William Montgomery, BM. (May 2, 1836) (CA)
William James to Jane Rentfro, Feb. 28, 1835.
Edward Duffee, BM. (Feb. 28, 1835) (CA, HRC)
Ezekeil John to Jane English, Oct. 17, 1835.
William Suthard, BM. (CA)
Thomas Johnston to Harriet G. Johnson, Sep. 7 (or Nov. 5),
1835. Henry Liggett, BM. (CA, HRC)
Charles King to Julia McElwee, Apr. 6, 1835.
E. G. Sevier, BM. (CA)
Thomas Kitchen to Margaret Bogart, Mar. 3, 1835.
(Mar. 3, 1835) (CA)
Elias Lane to Mahala Bowers, Feb. 17, 1835.
Littledery Johnston, BM. (HRC)
Thomas R. Lane to Malinda Cloud, May 13, 1835.
Joseph Lane, BM. (CA)
Nelson Lawrence to Louisa Cannon, June 21, 1835.
Hendison Yoakum, BM. (CA)
William Lea to Sarah Clark, Aug. 6, 1835.
John Clark, BM. (Aug. 6, 1835) (CA, HRC)
Nesbit Leonard to Elizabeth Burk, May 26, 1835.
Philip Beddo, BM. (CA)
Andrew Lilburn to Malena Cannon, Apr. 8, 1835.
Willis Short, BM. (CA)
Joseph N. Lore to Amanda Ashley, Apr. 16, 1835.
James H. Fain, BM. (CA)
Jacob Lowery to Kiziah Gossett, Jan. 3, 1835.
John W. Darnell, BM. (Jan. 3, 1835) (CA)
James Lynn to Nancy Dickson, Sep. 10, 1835.
James Bean, BM. (CA)
John G. Magill to Polly Lovelace, Oct. 22, 1835.
A. S. Lenoir, BM. (HRC)
James Manning to Rachel Kimbrell, May 15, 1835.
Peter Manning, BM. (CA)
Elijah Mason to Mary Gardner, Mar. 20, 1835.
Henry Liggett, BM. (Mar. __, 1835) (CA)
John A. Matheny to Lucinda Detherage, Nov. 19, 1835.
Abner Deatherage, BM. (Nov. 26, 1835) (CA, HRC)
George McNabb to Catherine Perkepile, Dec. 9, 1835.
John Blair, BM. (HRC)

Joseph Mee to Elizabeth Center, Apr. 8, 1835.
George L. Gallespie, BM. (CA)
Wesley Middleton to Polly Easter, Oct. 28 (or 29), 1835.
George W. Easter, BM. (CA, HRC)
John Mounds to Leah Brown, Oct. 31, 1835.
Samuel Margrave, BM. (CA)
Wade Narramore to Polly Tummins, July 4, 1835.
Pleasant Littleton, BM. (July 5, 1835) (CA)
James Neiper to Mary Ann Smith, Aug. 4, 1835.
George Weese, BM. (CA)
William Pearson to Mary McBath, Aug. 17, 1835.
_____ McBath, BM. (HRC)
Ruben Phillips to Anny Fike, Nov. 21, 1835.
(Nov. 22, 1835) (CA)
John Price to Nancy Luellen, Apr. 14, 1835.
Wm. Goodman, BM. (CA)
Hiram Raines to Catherine Davis, Apr. 8, 1835.
(Apr. 9, 1835) (CA)
William Rains to Jane McIntire, Mar. 25, 1835.
Isaac Rains, BM. (CA)
James R. Reagan to Mirah Lenoir, Aug. 31, 1835.
John Y. Smith, BM. (CA)
James P. Rector to Sarah Luttrell, Jan. 17, 1835.
James Eblen, BM. (CA)
Jeremiah Rich to Emily Bond, Oct. 2, 1835.
(HRC)
Henry Riche to Mary Box, Sep. 19, 1835.
Robert D. Duncan, BM. (CA)
Lewis M. Roberts to Mary Eleanor Stewart, Feb. 23, 1835.
John Shields, BM. (HRC)
James K. Robertson to Frances R. Lockett, Nov. 10, 1835.
John H. Wright, BM. (HRC)
William Silvey to Nancy Solomon, Nov. 11, 1835.
Jacob Lower (or Tower), BM. (Nov. 11, 1835) (CA, HRC)
Campbell Simpson to Elisa Boman, Aug. 17, 1835.
Elias Lane, BM. (HRC)
Wm. Snow to Mary Waller, Jan. 20, 1835.
Henry Liggett, BM. (Jan. 22, 1835) (CA)
James Stone to Mariline Browder, Mar. 11, 1835.
Manoah Stone, BM. (CA)
George W. Stout to Jane Greer, June 27, 1835.
William Davis, BM. (HRC)
Martin Strange to Louisa Russell, Dec. 31, 1835.
Henry Stegall, BM. (CA)
John H. Tally to Nancy Moore, July 27, 1835.
John Moore, BM. (CA)
John C. Terry to Matilda Christian, Nov. 5, 1835.
Hezekiah Love, BM. (HRC)
Abraham S. Thompson to Malinda Gibbons, Sep. 24, 1835.
Ralph Smith, BM. (CA)
Thomas J. Underwood to Maria Howard, Aug. 12, 1835.
George Gaines, BM. (HRC)
William Underwood to Elizabeth Young, Jan. 6, 1835.
Andrew McCullock, BM. (CA, HRC)

John Vann to Tabitha Williams, Aug. 13, 1835.
  Andrew McCullock, BM. (Jan. 7, 1835) (CA, HRC)
Adam Varner to Mary Ann Davidson, Sep. 14, 1835.
  Michael K. Selvage, BM. (Sep. 16, 1835) (CA)
Levi Voiles to Amy Shaw, June 8, 1835.
  _____ Driskill, BM. (June 11, 1835) (CA)
Abraham Weece (or Weese) to Polly Branham, Jan. 21, 1835.
  (HRC)
Samuel Weese to Rebecca Brackett, May 2, 1835.
  William Reese, BM. (HRC)
Solomon Weese to Polly Dennis, July 13, 1835.
  (May 2, 1835) (CA)
William Weese to Amanda J. Wester, Apr. 4, 1835.
  Absolom Tuttle, BM. (HRC)
John West to Jane Eldridge, Sep. 15, 1835.
  John Eldridge, BM. (HRC)
Benjamine Wiggins to Amanda M. Christian, Oct. 22, 1835.
  Philip Beddo, BM. (CA)
Robert Wilson to Eliza Scarbrough, Sep. 10, 1835.
  William Hapler, BM. (HRC)
Chesley Wright to Lavina Burnett, Sep. 20, 1835.
  Andrew Breazeale, BM. (CA)

1836

George Arnold to Nancy Cook, Oct. 11, 1836.
  Jonas R. Arnold, BM. (Oct. 13, 1836) (CA, HRC)
Morton Billingsley to Mahala Stubbs, July 23, 1836.
  Robert D. Cuncan, BM. (CA)
Charles Bottom to Matilda Rushen, Sep. 13, 1836.
  (Sep. 13, 1836) (CA)
Wm. H. Breazeale to Prathena Crumply, Jan. 13, 1836.
  Wm. Kitchen, BM. (Jan. 14, 1836) (CA)
John Burkett to Parmelia Burkett, Oct. 1, 1836.
  (HRC)
John Burry to Susan Mullins, Oct. 3, 1836.
  (Oct. 3, 1836) (CA)
Mark C. Capps to Delia Towers, Mar. 17, 1836.
  Gideon Capps, BM. (HRC)
Samuel Cate to Mary Qualls, Jan. 7, 1836.
  (Jan. __, 1836) (CA)
George Cook to Sattira Haggard, Sep. 2, 1836.
  John Cook, BM. (HRC)
Michael Cook to Ann Mullins, Apr. 8, 1836.
  (Apr. 10, 1836) (CA, HRC)
John A. Crockett to Nancy R. Patty, July 18, 1836.
  Gideon Dennis, BM. (July 29, 1836) (CA)
William Davis to Isabella Chilton, Mar. 7, 1836.
  (Mar. 7, 1836) (CA)
William Davis to Latha Johnston, Dec. 22, 1836.
  (Dec. 25, 1836) (CA)
Thomas Dearmond to Elizabeth Dearmond, Nov. 2, 1836.
  Wm. F. Brown, BM. (CA)
James Delozier to Matilda Tipton, May 28, 1836.
  (May 29, 1836) (CA)

Major M. Dobbins to Evangeline F. Miller, Apr. 7, 1836.
Ephraim Miller, BM. (no reference)
Abraham Dotson to Rhoda Mallacote, Jan. 2, 1836.
Samuel Dotson, BM. (CA)
William Driskill to Martha Johnston, Jan. 24, 1836.
Samuel S. Childress, BM. (Jan. 24, 1836) (CA, HRC)
Jesse Erwin to Peggy Hardin, AUg. 18, 1836.
James Willet, BM. (CA)
William Ewing to Malinda Alford, Sep. 14, 1836.
Robert Alford, BM. (CA)
John Ezell to Nancy Breazeale, Feb. 18, 1836.
Hancel B. Wright, BM. (CA)
Peter Finch to Amy Bledsoe, Dec. 29, 1836.
(Dec. 29, 1836) (CA)
Brittain (or Chastain) Freeman to Becky McMullin, Jan. 11,
1836. (Jan. 14, 1836) (CA, HRC)
Patrick Hartley to Lucy Ann Kincade, Oct. 28, 1836.
(Nov. 5, 1836) (CA)
Isaac Haynes to Issabella Carmichael, Nov. 22, 1836.
John Carmichael, BM. (CA)
Jesse Hays to Evaline Keith, Mar. 1, 1836.
Jeremiah R. Hays, BM. (Mar. 6, 1836) (CA, HRC)
Asa Hinds to Ruth Parks, Oct. 8, 1836.
(CA)
James Hoge to Katherine Mason, Nov. 22, 1836.
Robt. N. McEwin, BM. (CA)
William Hutson to Matilda B. Bright, Sep. 10, 1836.
Hansel B. Wright, BM. (Sep. 15, 1836) (CA)
Henry James to Celia Butler, Feb. 18, 1836.
(Feb. 18, 1836) (CA)
Anderson Jones to Frances Lewallen, Mar. 23, 1836.
Jesse Owings, BM. (HRC)
Henry Jones to Jane K. Watson, Nov. 24, 1836.
Josiah Montgomery, BM. (CA)
James Keeler to Betsey Green, June 26, 1836.
Wm. McReynolds, BM. (CA)
Joseph Lane to Rebecca Baldwin, Sep. 23, 1836.
Jesse Baldwin, BM. (HRC)
George W. Lower to Elvira Carter, Nov. 15, 1836.
John A. Sharp, BM. (Nov. 17, 1836) (CA)
James Lynn to Nancy Dickson, Sep. 10, 1836.
(HRC)
John Matlock to Mary McElwee, Mar. 28, 1836.
(Mar. 29, 1836) (CA)
Henry Monger to Nancy McKinny, Nov. 1, 1836.
(Nov. 1, 1836) (CA)
Nelson Munds to Anny Clark, July 11, 1836.
Austin L. Green, BM. (HRC)
William Nail to Jane Rankin, Dec. 28, 1837.
(Oct. 25, 1837) (CA)
Thomas Napier to Ethalinda Underwood, Aug. 11, 1836.
(Aug. 14, 1836) (CA, HRC)
Garland Powell to Sally Spraggins, Nov. 21, 1836.
John McDuffy, BM. (CA)

Henry (or Thomas) Purcy to May Ann Breden, Dec. 9, 1836.
(Dec. 15, 1836) (CA, HRC)
John J. Roberts to Nancy E. Gammon, Sep. 15, 1836.
Elijah Roberts, BM. (CA)
Elijah R. Robinson to Amelia Hardiman, Oct. 31, 1836.
(Nov. 2, 1836) (CA)
William Shackleford to Elizabeth Reeder, Sep. 25, 1836.
Edmund Pryor, BM. (HRC)
Richard Simpson to Martha E. Johnson, Oct. 20, 1836.
James P. Moon, BM. (CA)
Samuel Thompson to Margaret McKamey, Jan. 19, 1836.
William N. McKamey, BM. (HRC)
George Towers to Elvira Carter, Nov. 15, 1836.
John A. Sharp, BM. (HRC)
David Turpin to Dillia Wyatt, Mar. 23, 1836.
(HRC)
Henderson Wheat to Margaret Claibourn, Jan. 26, 1836.
Samuel Eblen, BM. (CA)
Roger Wilkey to Mariah West, Oct. 29, 1836.
Nimrod Newman, BM. (HRC)
Enoch Willett to Savilla A. Russell, Feb. 25, 1836.
Nathaniel Willett, BM. (Feb. 25, 1836) (CA, HRC)
John E. Williams to Polly Cofer, Jan. 29, 1836.
David Hood, BM. (CA)

1837

Mathew Allison to Mary J. Eblen, Oct. 15, 1837.
William Y. Driskill, BM. (CA)
Jacob Asher to Mary Bolin, Oct. 21, 1837.
William Warren, BM. (CA)
Robert Austen to Mary E. Merrick, Sep. 27, 1837.
John W. Robinson, BM. (Sep. 28, 1837) (CA)
Hezekiah Bacon to Lucinda Ballard, Aug. 12, 1837.
(Aug. 13, 1837) (CA)
John Bailey to Sarah Barry, Dec. 13, 1837.
(Dec. 13, 1837) (CA)
George Bowers to Mary Armstrong, Nov. 7 (or Jan. 2), 1837.
(CA)
Hugh G. Boyd to Mary Staples, Aug. 21, 1837.
Robert Clark, BM. (CA)
Hugh L. Breazeale to Amanda M. King, Feb. 15, 1837 (or
1827). (_____, 1837) (CA)
William Brown to Polly Weese, Mar. 3, 1837.
Solomon Easter, BM. (CA)
Henry F. Carter to Elenor Walker, Jan. 16, 1837.
(Jan. 18, 1837) (CA)
Thomas Coffer to Jane Martin, Nov. 7, 1837.
William Martin, BM. (Nov. 7, 1837) (CA, HRC)
James Deatherage to Nancy Jane Sparks, Apr. 5, 1837.
Phelomon Edgemond, BM. (CA)
Archibald M. Evans to Caroline Liggett, Oct. 3, 1837.
Robt. D. Duncan, BM. (Oct. 5, 1837) (CA)
Nathaniel Gist to Nancy Homes, Sep. 16, 1837.
James Householder, BM. (Sep. 16, 1837) (CA)

James Haley to Mary Clark, Nov. 22, 1837.
  Thomas McElwee, BM. (Nov. 23, 1837) (CA)
John W. Hudson to Elizabeth Howard, Oct. 12, 1837.
  John W. Butler, BM. (CA)
James Isham to Elizabeth Williams, Sep. 23, 1837.
  Nimrod Underwood, BM. (Sep. 24, 1837) (CA)
Berry Johnson to Sarah Rentfro, Apr. 15, 1837.
  William Johnson, BM. (CA)
Francis J. Johnson to Lucinda Johnson, Aug. 11, 1837.
  (Aug. 17, 1837) (CA)
John Johnson to Rebecca Davis, Nov. 21, 1837.
  (Nov. 26, 1837) (CA)
James Jones to Polly Sellers, Oct. 28, 1837.
  (CA)
Gilbery Lawhorn to Sarah Shadwick, July 18, 1837.
  George Arnold, BM. (CA)
William Locket to Clarrissa Liles, Apr. 8, 1837.
  Willis Locket, BM. (CA)
George Mitchell to Kiziah Casey, Oct. 5, 1837.
  Mathew P. McEwen, BM. (Oct. 5, 1837) (CA)
Jones P. Moon to Lucinda C. Johnson, Oct. 20, 1837.
  Richard Simpson, BM. (Oct. 26, 1837) (CA)
Caswell Allen Niper to Anney King, Sep. 2, 1837.
  William Griffine, BM. (Sep. 9, 1837) (CA, HRC)
Henry W. Pickle to Elizabeth Tarner, Dec. 7, 1837.
  (Dec. 7, 1837) (CA)
Samuel Ramsey to Martha Leake, July 20, 1837.
  J. W. McCullough, BM. (HRC)
Humphrey Rector to Hatty Talliferro, June 22, 1837.
  (June 23, 1837) (CA)
Samuel Reed to Mary Ann Barnett, Nov. 4, 1837.
  William Neill, BM. (CA)
John Riggs to Elizabeth Piercy, Sep. 23, 1837.
  Andrew H. English, BM. (CA)
James Scabrough to Ann Davis, Nov. 16, 1837.
  Jonathan Shannan, BM. (Nov. 16, 1837) (CA)
Richard Simpson to Martha E. Johnson, Oct. 20, 1837.
  (Oct. 26, 1837) (CA, HRC)
Millican Stephenson to Malinda Breazeale, July 13, 1837.
  William Childress, BM. (CA)
William Swafford to Elizabeth McDuffee, Sep. 5, 1837.
  Anguish McDuffee, BM. (CA)
Nathaniel Turner to Susanah McPherson, Sep. 11, 1837.
  Nathanial Haggard, BM. (Sep. 12, 1837) (CA)
John Umphries to Patient (or Patience) Richards, Aug. 31,
  1837. Richard Watt, BM. (Sep. 3, 1837. (CA, HRC)
William Weese to Rachel Dennis, Dec. 8, 1837.
  John Brown, BM. (CA)
John Williams to Mahaley Jane Stennett, Nov. 22, 1837.
  Martin Williams, BM. (HRC)
Bobby Winten to Susan F. Jackson, Dec. 20, 1837.
  John Gent, BM. (Dec. 21, 1837) (CA)

1838

Abraham Howard to Kezziah Thrailkill, Apr. 15, 1838.
  (HRC)

INDEX

Abeel, Rachel 41
Abels, Fanny 4
  John M. 45
Able, Barbara 46
  David 66
  Elizabeth 61
  Francis 45
  John 49
  Joseph 61
  Mary A. 66
Acard, John 24
Acord, Cornelius 32
  Cornelius (Jr.) 32
  Cornelius (Sr.) 32
  Creesy 32
  David 32
  Joseph 34, 37
Adaems, Sally 44
Adair, William 9
Adams, Dianah 5
  Francis 59
  John 40
  Nelson A. 63
  Sally 60
Adcock, Archibald 32
  Tyra 32
Adkins, Charles 43
  Gabriel 20
Adkinson, Abraham (Also see
    Adkison, Absolom) 18
  James 29
  Sally (Also see Adkison)
    18
Adkison, Absolom (Also see
    Adkinson, Abraham) 18
  Alexander 45
  David 18
  Sally (also see Adkinson)
    18
Adkisson, Absolom 60
  Terry 63
Ahart, Elizabeth 56
  George 65
Aikens, James 61

Aldridg, Francis 40
Alexander, Esther 62
  James 56
  Margaret 24
  Mary E. 39
  Russell 9
  Samuel 48
  William 23
Alford, John 65
  Malinda 70
  Robert 70
Alif, Polly 42
Allen, Betsey 17
  Carington 45
  Covington 32
  Elias 7, 9
  Ellizabeth 4
  John 6, 11
  Kiziah 26, 31
  Lorenda 62
  Loretta Jane 65
  Robert 52
  Ruben 51, 58
  Sally 57
  William 45
  Wm. C. 5
Allens(?), Nancy 53
Allin, Betsey 7
Allison, ? 38
  Amy 4
  Betsy 25
  Caty 4
  Henson 37
  Jinny 11
  Letitia 31
  Mathew 71
  Nancy 53
  Polly 4
  Robert 29
  Susanah 5
  Uriah 4, 11, 18, 23, 26,
    27, 28, 29, 32, 41
Allsup, James 16
Ally, David 33

Ambrose, David 45
Amos, Lucinda 51
  Mary 44
  Rhoda 62
Anarew, Samuel 31
Anderson, Henry 16
  Issac 27, 29
  Mathew 29
  Michael 30, 37, 40
  Stephen 27
  Thomas 11
  William 11, 40, 49
Andrews, Samuel 38
Anthony, Catherine 49
  Elizabeth 39
  Lewis 50
Applegate, Nathaniel 14, 16
Arbuckle, Catherine H. 13
Archer, Aron 45
  Moses 7
Arnold, George 20, 29, 49, 61, 65,
  69, 72
  Jonas 16, 23, 28
  Jonas R. 69
  Michael 30, 51
  William 24
Arms, Hezekiah 47
Armstrong, Abel 32
  Mary 71
Arsterton, Catey 30
Asher, Charles 32
  Elizabeth 61
  Jacob 71
  Leonard 32
  Thomas 55
Ashley, Amanda 67
  Joseph 28
  Noah 9, 10, 17, 20, 26, 38
Atkinson, Nancy 49
Atmer, Mary 10
Ault, Henry 52
  Mary 36
  Peggy 39
Ausbern, James 37
Austen, Ann 8
  Robert 71
Averett, Jesse 34
Avery, Becky 2
  John 13
  Peter 2, 13
Ayer, Eliza (also see Ayers) 9
  John 49
  Maria (also see Burnett) 56
  Zacheus 56
Ayers, Alexander 45

Ayers (cont.)
  Eliza (also see Ayer) 9
  Peggy 17
  Zacheus 5, 56
  Zarhariah 53
Ayhart, George 57
Bacon, Drewy A. 61
  Hezekiah 71
  Joshiah I. 59
  Lowery A. 59
  Washington 40
Bagwell, Jonathan 56
  Sally 54
Bailey, Ann 19
  Daniel 16, 22
  Isaac 3, 51
  James 10
  John 71
  Levina 15
  Patsey 51, 57
  Pleasant 61
  William 20, 22, 32
Baily, Jane 26
Baker, Ann 64
  Betsey 8, 23
  Elijah 24, 27
  Isaac 19
  Jacob 37, 38
  James 29
Baldwin, Francis 54
  Francis J. 49
  Jesse 65, 70
  Rebecca 70
Ball, David 61
Ballard, Caroline 61
  Elizabeth 37, 50
  Francis 62
  Lucinda 71
  Lucy 45
  Mary 43, 53
  Rebecca 35
  Washington 59
  William 6, 45, 50, 53, 55
Balton, Allen 48
Bandy (?), Cintha 34
Bane, Arthur 24
Bankin, Samuel S. 3
Barger, John 22
  Isaac 40, 49
Bargor, Isaac 41
Barksdale, Stephen 63
Barnard, Samuel 29, 30
Barnell, William 3
Barnett, Cilly 10
  Elizabeth 9

Barnett (cont.)
Huldah 65
John 27
Martha 51
Mary 23
Mary Ann 72
Wiley 66
Wm. 2
Barns, William H. 52
Barrow, Martha 41
Barry, Hyram (also see Berry) 34
Keziah (also see Berry) 21
Sarah 71
Bartly, Easter 2
Barton, Gilbreath 17
Gillesreath 21
Bashears, Betsy 10
Robert 7
Basket, Wm. W. 50
Baskin, Rosey 3, 5
Bassenger (?), Jacob 32
Battam, Allen (also see Bolton)
40
Bazil, Samuel 13
Bean, James 67
Beatty, Hugh 3
Beavers, James 9, 27
Wm. 27
Beaverz, James 24
Beckett, Charles 2
Becknal, Betsey (also see Bucknel)
34
Beddo, Philip 27, 56, 64, 66, 67,
69
Bedo, Philip 57
Bedwell (Esq.) 40
Hiram 40
Beeman, Wm. 13
Belew, John 32
Bell, Abigail 38
Abigall 43
David N. 65
Thomas 40
Bellard, Susan 40
Bendy, Charlotte 28
Benton, Francis (also see Frencis
Benton) 27, 37
Frencis (also see Francis
Benton) 27
Berry, Ann 61
Hyram (also see Barry) 34
Keziah (also see Barry) 21
Peter 6
Polly 39
Sally 55

Berry (cont.)
Volly 65
William 27, 45
William C. 52
William W. 32
Wm. W. 29
Besher, Jerimia 52
Bevely, Jane 50
Beverly, Wm. 47
Bibe, Thomas 4
Bigham, William 6
Billingsley, Morton 69
Bird, Caty 6
Birdwell, Joshua 14
Moses 14
Bishop, Masey 65
Nancy 53
Black, Alexander 47
Elizabeth 54
John 12, 14, 56
William G. 32
Blackburn, Paul 14
Blackston, Robert 55
Thomas 9
Blackwell, Armstead 29
Elizabeth 19
George 37
Hugh 65
Mary 5
Richard 37
Sally 6, 30
Blair, Allen 50
Elizabeth 42
Hugh 63
Isabella 26
James 26
John 42, 45, 67
Rachel 35
William 2
Blake, Fanny 24
Larkin H. 63
Mary 35
Sarah 37
Thomas 29, 43
Thos. 37
William 63
William G. 38, 43
Blanton, Abner 24
Rebecca 52
Bledsoe, Amy 70
Blevins, Polly 51
Usley 40
Wm. 63
Blythe, Thomas G. 65
Boake, William S. 40

Boden, Jinny 22
Bogart, Ab'm 13
   Abraham 27, 29, 34, 40, 52
   Charles 52, 56
   Elizabeth 61
   Henry 38, 40
   Margaret 67
   Nancy 29
   Sarah 62
   Solomon 44
   William 13, 27
Bolden, Fielding 16
Bolin, Mary 71
Bolton, Allen (also see Battam)
   40
Boman, Elisa 68
Bomar, William W. 32
Bond, Emily 68
   Melisa 47
Bonds, Barbary Ann 41
Bonigan, Smith 16
Booker, Haram 59
Booth, Pheby 59
   Rachel 59
   William 43
Boothe, Aron 59
   Ruth 59
Booths, Hannah 59
Bottom, Charles 69
Bower, James 18, 25, 51
   John 34
   John W. 16
   Patsey 25
   Richard 7
   William 16
Bowers, Betsy 26
   George 71
   James 16, 24, 54
   John 24, 35
   John W. 12
   Kitty 11
   Mahala 67
Bowling, Levina 67
Bowman, Edward 56
   George 40
   James 12
   John 10, 18
   Lewis 43, 44
   Nancy 10
   Sally 21, 43
   Samuel 43, 49
   Susanah 10
   William 14, 29
Box, Mary 68
   Nancy 27

Boxer, Mary K. 62
Boyd, Angelina 59
   Hugh G. 71
   Willaim 61
Bozeman, Thomas 3
Bracket, Nancy 55
Brackett, Burrel 52
   John 63
   Permelia 63
   Rebecca 69
Bradley, Samuel 7
Brahen, Martha 41
Branan, George 40
   Jefferson 37
   Nancy 40
Brandon, Adam 34, 37, 42,
   Ann 42
   George 45
   John 59, 63
   Philip 34, 37
Branham, Agnes 35
   Berthena 51
   George 25
   Jane 38
   John 49
   Linsey 65
   Livingston 46
   Lois 51
   Malakiah 61
   Malinda 64
   Nelly 22
   Noah 61
   Pleasant 23
   Polly 69
   Richard 20
   Sally 15
   Talton 14
   Tarlton 20
   Thomas 22, 58
   William 32, 41, 56
Brannam, William 47
Brannen, Livingston (also see
   Branum) 32
Brannum, Pleasant 24
   William 52
Branum, Livingston (also see
   Brannen) 32
Brashear, Bazel 5
   Sally 17
   Samuel 18
   Walter 18
Brasheare, Joseph (also see
   Breashear) 53
Brasher, Loman (?) 34
Brashears, Betsey 7, 9

Brown (cont.)
Thomas 2, 14, 22, 25, 27, 30, 63
Thos. 29
William 4, 6, 7, 14, 15, 19, 21, 45, 56, 71
Wm. 13
Wm. F. 69
Bruce, G. W. 29
Green M. 24
Brumley, Elizabeth 58
Bryan, George W. 34
Wm. 38
Bryant, Ambrose 6
Jane 16
John H. 56
Joseph 24
Lewis 44
Little B. 12
Polly 14, 24
Priscilla 45
Sisannah 55
Buchanan, Hercules 32
James 12, 27
Jeminia 10
Jennie 9
Jeremiah 7, 13
Mary 23
Rebecca 6
Sarah 30
Buchannan, Susanna 13
Buckalow, Catherine 48
Buckhannon, James 40
Bucklen, Joanna 23
Bucknel, Betsey (also see Becknal) 34
Henry 34
Buford, John 5
Bullar, Isaac 10
Bullard, Isaac 54
Bundum, Perlitha 60
Burch, Phillip 6
Burdwell, Joshua 9
Burgis, William 6
Burk, Charlie 10
Elizabeth 67
Hepsiby 58
James 13
Milton 37, 49
Peggy 23
Polly 39
Robert 1, 7
Sarah 65
Susan 46
Burnett, David 56

Burnett (cont.)
Dolly Brunetta 66
Elizabeth 28, 38
Jefferson 57
Jerima 66
John 66, 69
Judiah 62
Lavina 69
Lucinda 29
Maria (also see Ayer) 56
Maryana 28
Moses 14
Parmelia 69
Patsy 56
Polly 33, 35
Sally 44
Samuel 27
Stacey 14
Burns, James 66
Jinny 20
Laird 66
Mary 2
Burris, Isaac 45, 46, 52, 64
Lewis 30, 40, 48
Stephen 32
William 7
William H. 66
Burry, John 69
Bush, Robert 24
Bussle, William 37
Butler, Celia 70
Elias 27
Gidean 43
Jacob 34
John W. 72
Phebe 10
Pheby 43
Rhody 32
Thomas 34
Walter 43
Byrd, Jesse 3, 4
Joseph 20, 25, 31, 35, 47, 57
Nancy 29
William B. 53
Byrdwell, Patsey 37
Cain, Robert B. 51
Caldwell, Wm. 2
Callison, Nancy 3
Campbell, Christine 61
James 66
John 49, 59
Robert 20
William 2
Cane, Dicy 40
James 43

Cane (cont.)
  William 40
Cannon, Betsey 19
  Eveline 63
  Louisa 67
  Malena 67
  Patsey 45
  Robert 41
  Samuel 44
  Thomas 14
Capps, Carson 63
  Gideon 69
  Mark C. 69
  Nancy 66
  Sarah 61
Caps, Moses 40, 43
Car, Catherine E. 46
  William 3
Card, Richard)also see Curd) 25
Carden, James 44
  Sally 23
Cardwell, Elizabeth 58
  Mary 33
Carmicel, Cornelius 45
Carmichael, Alex 2
  Alexander 2
  Issabella 70
  Jane 31, 51
  John 16, 45, 70
Carmichal, Alexander 2
Carrack, Addeson 32, 43
Carrick, Addison 37, 39, 43
Carroll, Alfred 63
  Elizabeth 45
  Hiram 66
  Susanna 29
  William 34, 35, 56
Carson, Adam 11
  Betsey 31
  Nancy 20
  Wilson 66
Cart, Polly 25
Carter, Ann 1
  Caleb 43
  Elvira 70, 71
  George 20
  Henry F. 71
  James 66
  Jesse 27, 34, 47
  Jinney 13
  Joseph 66
  Marcus 40
  Micijah 1
  Moses L. 56, 66
  Philip 53

Carter (cont.)
  Rachel 9, 51
  Robert 45
  (?), Susan 43
  Susana 40
  Susanna 26
  Thomas 45
Casey, Abner 9, 12
  Alexander 14, 20
  Ambler 13
  Anthony 16
  Barbara 16
  Hetty 50
  Jane 37
  Jesse 20
  Joshua 47
  Kiziah 72
  Levi 37, 53
  Mary 12
  Pleasant 53
  Susannah 42
Cash, Betsey 48
  Judy 52
Casner, Isaac 20
  Jacob 18
Cassey, Alexander 2
Casteel, Barney 27
  Caleb 20
  Edmond 23
  John 6
  Mary 23
  Zachariah 22
Cate, Ephraim 40
  Samuel 69
Cates, Benjamine 47
  Ephraim 43
Catlet, Sally 54
Caves, William (also see Cavy) 27
Cavett, Moses 13
  Sally 3
Cavy, William (also see Caves) 27
Cawood, Jacob 63
Center, Caroline 46
  Elizabeth 68
  Eveline 52
  Francis K. 34
  James 21
  Lindy 31
  Martin (also see Milton Center) 28
  Milton (also see Martin Center) 5, 28
  Polly 21
  Seaborn 20
  Susan 36

Center (cont.)
  Willis S. 45
Cery, John 4
Chambers, George 66
Chamblee, Sally 22
Chaney, John I. 53
Channy, John I. 63
Cherokees, Suckie (also see
    Walker) 10
Childers, Nancy (also see
    Childres) 18
Childres, Nancy (also see
    Childers) 18
  Thomas C. 22
Childress, Mossy Ann 36
  Samuel 61, 62
  Samuel L. 51, 63
  Samuel S. 70
  Thomas 24
  Thos. C. 21
  William 72
Childs, Elizabeth 15
  Pheby 16
Chiles, Rowland 30
Chilton, Isabella 69
Christenberry, Esther 58
  Ginny 4
  Joshua 1
  William 55
Christian, Amanda M. 69
  Francis 60
  Gilbert 40
  Matilda 68
  Walter 50, 63
Christianberry, Greene 47
Chumley, Claibourn 64
Churchill, Harriet 19
Ciscow, Isaac 16
Cizire, ? 18
Claibourn, Margaret 71
Clark, Anny 70
  Betsey 23
  Charles 25
  Chas. L. 64
  Featerson 47
  John 27, 67
  John G. 53
  John W. 25
  Joseph M. 35
  Mary 72
  Matilda V. 58
  Polly (also see Martin) 7, 33,
    56
  Richard 49
  Robert 71

Clark (cont.)
  Ruthy 36
  Sarah 28, 61, 67
  Sarah P. 51
  Susan B. 42
  Thomas 20
  Thomas N. 55, 58
  Thos. N. 52
  William 45
Claunch, David 18
Cleck, Betsey (also see Click) 17
Clemmons, Rayne 37
Clenny, Jonathan 9
Click, Anna 8
  Betsey (also see Cleck) 17
  James 61
  Peter 10
  William 20
Clift, Polly 32
  William 37, 64
Cloud, Patsy 53
  Malinda 67
Clough, Robert 40
Clowar, Jacob 53
Clower, Daniel 47
  James 53
Clowney, Esther A. 58
  Martha Montgomery 60
Cluck, Henry 45
  William 45
Coady, Charles 11
  Nancy 13
Coatney, Elizabeth 12
  William 12
Cob, Abigal (also see Cole) 46
Cobb, Asa 13, 31
  Deborah 19
  Mahulda 27
  Polly 31
Cody, Arthur (also see Coody) 20
  Charles 11
  Rachel 7
Coe, Patsey 20
Cofer, Fanny 60
  James 45, 49
  Nancy 38
  Polly 71
  Thomas 64
Coffer, Thomas 71
Cole, Abigal (also see Cob) 46
  Eliza 39
  Elizabeth 62
Coleman, Martha 58
  Mary 2
Colier, Patsey 28

Collier, David 5
  Elizabeth E. 38
  Elly 29
  John 53
  Lucinda G. 34
Collins, Jincy 41
  Katherine 48
  Solomon 30
Combs, Lewis 16
Condon, John 1, 4
Conk, Mahaly M. 28
Connelly, Enoch 12
Coodey, Charles 10
Coody, Arthur (also see Cody) 20
  Elizabeth 3
  James 25
Cook, Barbara 34
  Catherine 50
  George 14, 69
  John 50, 59, 69
  John H. 66
  Mary 20
  Michael 69
  Nancy 69
  Nisy 59
  Ruben 54
  Rubin 45
  Sally 26
  William S. 34
Cooley, Betsey 65
  Permelia 65
  Rebecca 34
Cooly, James 34, 49, 53
  John 56
  Joshua 32
  Lucinda 29
  Nancy 27
Cooper, Azarah 29
  Azariah 9, 24
  James 14
  Malinda 25
  Mary 2
  Richard 5
  Richard A. 6
  Robert 35
  Sally 56
Copeland, Ambrose 32
  Jesse 64
  John 59
  Polly 48
  Solomon 25
Copher, Abraham 49
  Lemson 27
  Polly 25
Copland, Solomon 34

Coppage, Thomas 25
Cordwell, Kissiah 47
Corey, Mary 12
Cornealison, William 25
Cosby, James 56
Couch, Ann 12
Coulson, John 25
Coulter, Caty 5
  John 5
Council, Howard L. 34
Councill, Isaac 5
Coupland, Lyda 4
Cove, John 46, 50
Covington, William 50
Cox, Alexander 30
  Isham 4, 26
  James 22
  John 56
  Joshua 12
  Mary (also see Nancy Cox) 27
  Mary Ann 65
  Nancy (also see Mary Cox) 27
  Nathaniel 8
  Polly 40
  Richard 58
  Sally 40
  Samuel 48
  Thomas 20, 37
  Thos. 38
Cozby, James 14
Crag, Adam 9
Cragen, Elendor 45
Craig, David 18
  John 14
  Thomas 9
Craige, James 4
Craven, Martha H. 59
Cravens, Eliza 61
  Margaret H. 42
Cravet, Betsey 27
Crawford, Robert 12
Crenshaw, John 50
Crevan, Ann 51
Crevat, Moses 50
Crew, James 37, 64
Crisp, Elizabeth 29
  James 29, 45
  Rhoda 14
Crockett, John A. 69
Cross, Benjamin L. (also see
    Crow) 35
Crouch, James 4
Crow, Alexander 35
  Ana (also see Ann Crow) 56
  Ann (also see Ana Crow) 56

Crow (cont.)
Benjamin L. (also see Cross)
35
Betsey 18
Edward 20
Elizabeth 53
George 6, 17
James 66
James Lewis 14
John 34, 35
Nancy 26, 49
Patsy 66
Polly 24
Rachel 22
Robert 40, 42
William (also see Willis Crow)
25, 32
Willis (also see William Crow)
25, 32
Wm. 47
Crowder, John 54
Sarah 66
Crumbliss, Alice 15
Hugh 9, 10
James 15, 27, 31
Crumply, Prathena 69
Culp, Harmon 18
Peggy 11
Culvehouse, Edward 37
Cuncan, Robert D. 69
Cunningham, John 59
Rhoday 29
Valentine 37, 58
Curd, Richard (also see Card) 25
Curtis, Rebecca 18
DeRossett, Lewis 25
William 27
Dalb, David 9
Daley, Polly 17
Dalton, Bradley 20, 22
Elizabeth 54
James 32, 46
Sally 18
Thomas 30
Danforth, Josiah 53
Daniel, John 38
Nancy 41
Nathan 20
Patsey 28
Darnell, John W. 65, 67
Daugherty, Barbary 33
Dauret, John 12
Davenport, David 18
David, Abraham 18
Azariah 5

David (cont.)
Owen 5
Davidson, Henry 43, 55
John 45
Mary Ann 69
Sally 2
William 43
Davis, Alexander 53, 59
Alfred 12
Andrew 66
Ann 72
Anna 43
Asa 20, 34
Bazzil 3
Brittain 29, 43
Catherine 42, 68
Charles 63
Dravy 61
Edward 38
Elizabeth 34
Fanny 29
George 59, 63
James 13
John 38, 40, 48, 50
Judith 6
Julian 55
Litha 63
Nancy 12
Nathan 66
Nathaniel L. 56
Owen 64
Polly 6, 41, 56
Rebecca 35, 72
Sally 12, 27
Samuel 21, 31, 43, 66
Samuel C. 38
Sucky 3
William 1, 56, 68, 69
Dawson, Elizabeth 54
Mary Ann 53
Silas 53, 64
Day, John 66
Samuel 66
William 43
Deakins, Townley 3, 15
Dean, David 6, 56
Dearmond, Easther 45
Elizabeth 69
Grizzy B. 66
James 1, 11, 18
John 66
Samuel J. 66
Thomas 69
Deatherage, Abner 35, 67
James 56, 71

Duncan (cont.)
  Sarah 27
Dunigan, Daniel 54
Dunkin, Benjamine 38
Dunlap, D. G. 41
  Eady 9
  Hugh 32
  Susan K. 36
  W. C. 39
  William 13, 47
Dunn, Elizabeth 32
Dunningham, Peggy 20
Dunwold, Charlotte 65
Dupee, Betsey 63
Durham, Cealy 47
Durne, Daniel 3
Durret, Martin 23
Durrett, John 23
  Martin 23, 32
  Willias 16
  Willis 25, 49
Dyke, John 57, 59
Eakins, Absolom 9
Earle, Archibald 30
  Thomas 30
Early, Frederick 35
  Thomas 35
Earp, Richardson 56
Easely, Judy 34
Easly, Juda 31
East, John 55
  John T. 48
Easter, Ellinor 39
  George W. 68
  Peter 32
  Polly 68
  Solomon 53, 71
Easton, John (also see Eaton) 56
Eaton, Jane 43
  Jenney 18
  Jenny 18
  John (also see Easton) 53, 56
  Joshua 32
  Lucy 14
Eblen, Edward 9
  Eliza 14, 52
  James 68
  James G. 63
  John 25, 32, 46
  Keziah 42
  Mary J. 71
  Nancy 34
  Polly 6
  Samuel 21, 71
  Sarah 6

Eblen (cont.)
  William 6, 12, 17, 40, 44, 51
Eblin, Ann 16
  Levina 15
Eddington   , James 10
Edgemond, Phelomon 71
Edgman, Johnston 53
  William 53
Edminston, John 27
  William 27
Edmond, Mathew 14
Edmonds, Levisey (also see
  Edwards) 14
Edmonston, Samuel 48
Edwards, Edward 52, 57
  Isabella 54
  John 19, 67
  Levisey (also see Edmonds) 14
  William 33
Eldridge, Benjamin 17, 25
  Elizabeth 11
  Jane 69
  Jefferson 35
  Jesse 4, 35
  John 69
  Katy 14
  Nancy (also see Etheridge) 2,
    13, 30, 41
  Peggy 12
  Polly 17, 25
  Sampson 2
  Samuel 2
  Simpson 4
  Thomas 17
  Westley 50
Elkins, Betsey 11
  Jacob 21
  John 35
  Lydia 36
  Mary Ann 27
Ellender, Janes
Ellinder, Jane 53
Ellis, Anna 48
  Betsey 33
  Calib 57
  Charles 57, 64
  Espere 22
  Francis 35
  John 6, 66
  Joseph 48
  Polly 29
  William 33, 48, 55, 57, 59, 63
Ellison, Elizabeth 13
  James 50
  Polly 9

Emery, Malinda 16
Eness, William (Also see Enoss or
   Inness) 33
England, Isaac 20, 21
   John 13
   Lucinda 12
   Petina 60
   Prudance 38
   Thomas 21, 57
English, Andrew 46
   Andrew H. 72
   Jane 67
Enoss, William (also see Eness or
   Inness) 33
Ervin, Anna 33
Erwin, Esther 63
   Frances (also see Francis
     Erwin) 16
   Francis (also see Frances
     Erwin) 16
   Hannah 33
   Jesse 70
   Margaret 21
   Polly 11
   Samuel 30
   William 23, 35
Eskridge, Samuel 43
Essary, Anna 29
   Elizabeth 34
   John 29
Essery, John 4, 14
   Patsey 11
Estes, John W. 17
Etheridge, Charity 39
   Michael (also see Ethridge) 27
   Nancy (also see Eldridge) 41
Ethridge, Michael (also see
   Etheridge) 27
Evans, Abby 30
   Archibald M. 71
   Arden 11
   Benjamin 5, 10
   Betsey 2, 28
   Betsy 49
   Elijah 8
   Elizabeth C. 66
   Evan 36
   Francis M. 57
   Jeremiah 12
   Nancy 11, 31, 48
   Nancy D. 64
   Patrick 58
   Polly 5
   Rubin 40
   Samuel 43

Evans (cont.)
   Willis 38, 47, 64
Ewell, Jane 54
Ewin, James 35
Ewing, Arthur 35, 44
   Francis 62
   Jacob 35
   Joseph 33
   Samuel H. 53
   Sarah 51
   William 70
Ewings, Anna 48
Ezell, John 70
   Levi 46
   Milly 36
Fagan, Mary 3
Fain, James H. 67
   Margaret 55
Fairchilds, Lewis 21
Falton, Martha 46
Faries, Richard 16
Farman, Thomas 35
Farmer, Elijah 17
   Elizabeth 39
   Nancy 53
Fell, James 50
Felts, Archilees 53
Ferguson, Martha 15
   Sarah 23
   T. L. 60
Field, Sally 17
Fielder, Jeremiah 12
Fields, Jenny 22
   Jeremiah 12
   Jeremich 18
   Lansford 24
   Thomas 13
Fifer, John (also see Tifer) 38
Fike, Anny 68
   Josiah 25, 30, 33
   Mary 33
   Nancy 29
   Sophia 48
Finch, Peter 70
Findley,(?) 53
   Mary 4
Findly, George 38
Finley, John 66
   Samuel 38
Finly, Mary 60
   Peggy 60
Fisher, Noah 64
Flat, John 2
Flatt, Benjamin 5
   James 16, 17

Fleener (?), Abraham 35
  Henry 33, 66
Fleiner, Betsy 41
Flenner, Susan 35
Forbish, Alexander 9
Ford, Edmond (also see Edward
    Ford) 43
  Edward (also see Edmond Ford)
    43
  James 43
  Sally 14
Foreman, Elijah 17
Forester, Larkin 41
Formwalt, John 6
Forrester, Alex 39
  Alexander 21
  James 1, 14
  Larkin 35
  Mary 32
  Samuel P. 57
  Solomon 28
  Thomas 18
Forshee, Betsy 9
Fort, Stephen (Sen.) 46
Foshall, Phillip 5
Foshee, Abraham 40
  Betsey 24
  Drusilla 18
  John A. 25
Foster, Eliza 58
Fouche, Nancy 8
Fouste, Joab 53
Fout, Julia 29
  Julian 27
  William D. 38
Foute, Charlotte 36
  William L. 64
Frances, Hugh 6
Francis, Elizabeth 35
  Hugh 5, 6, 12, 40
  James 59
  John Wood 66
  Nancy 40
  Polly 6
  Susanna 32
  Woodson 3
Frazier, Jane 42
Freeman, Brittain (also see
    Chastain Freeman) 70
  Chastain (also see Brittain
    Freeman) 70
  James 30, 38, 43, 50, 62
  James Madison 59
  John 3
  Littleton 64

Freeman (cont.)
  Sylvester 48
Fritts, David 50
  George 40
  Henry 40, 57, 66
  Jacob 23
  John 23
  Peter 53
  Philip 53, 56
Fritz, Peter 41
Fryar, Thomas 50
Frost, Nancy 20
Fulcher, Frances 5
Fuller, Abraham 48, 57
  George 61
  Nancy 46
Fulton, Rebecca 28
  Thomas 3
Funderburk, Catherine 49
Funk, Essau 57
  Isaac 23
  Jacob 53
  John 30
  Kitty 25
  Nancy 39
  Susanna 23
Gable, Israel 9
Gaines, George 68
Gains, Fanny 23
  George W. 55
Galbraith, Wm. 62
Galbreath, Alexander 10, 46
  William 20, 30, 51, 52, 57
  Wm. 50, 62
Gallaher, Abraham 51
  Benj. H. 41
  Elizabeth 19
  George 35, 50
  Harris B. 33
  James 2, 10, 43
  James A. 34
  James H. 28
  Janey M. 45
  Jinny 17
  Lucinda 34
  Nancy 9, 51
  Nancy A. 34
  Polly 10
  Robert 19
  Thomas 17, 35
  William 2
  Wyatt 18, 25
Gallaway, James 35
Gallbreath, Thomas 4
Gallespie, George L. 68

Gallion, Abraham 36
  Isaac 54
  Patsey 36
  Rachel 54
Galloway, Ann 50
  Betsey 29
  Ginny 3
  James 3
  Jesse 28, 29, 30, 45
  Levi 28, 35
  Nancy 30
  Patsey 6
  William S. 54
Gallyon, Isaac 43
Galyon, Abraham 41
Gambell, John 2
Gamble, Betsey G. 54
  James (also see Gambrill) 46,
    51, 66
  Polly 54
  Robert 30
Gambrill, James (also see Gamble)
Gammon, Elizabeth 34
  Mahala 56
  Nancy E. 71
  William 48
Gann, Abraham 46
  Nathan 21
Gardener, Barbara 22
  Thomas 53
Gardenhire, Adam 14
  G. W. 30
  George 43
  George W. 36
  Margaret 40
  Mathew 28
  William 2, 12, 22
Gardner, James 22
  Mary 67
  Nancy (also see Garner) 29
  Thomas 47, 50
  William H. 50
  Wm. H. 55
Garner, Nancy (also see Gardner)
    29
Garrett, Elizabeth 50
  Nancy 21
  Sally 33, 48
  Synthea 20
  Synthia 21
Gaunt, John 12
Gay, Curly 33
  William 30, 33
Gennings, John (also see Gunning)
    43

Gent, John 72
  Josiah 8, 59
Gentry, Owing 48
  Shadrick 41
Geren, Lidia 58
  Sally 10
  Samuel 10
Getgood, Alexander 54
Ghent, Charlotte 64
Gibbons, Elizabeth 65
  Malinda 68
Gibson, Caleb 60
  Drusilla 50
  Isaac 10
  James 66
  John 50
  Jonathan 38
  Reubin 46
  Shedrick 35
Gideon, Mary W. 65
Gilbert, Alexander 46
  Archibald 57
  Benjamine 64
  Pleasant 30
  William 59
Gilbreath, Alexander 46
  Elizabeth 43
  William 21
Giles, William 66
Gillan, William 17
Gilliland, Robert 18, 32
  Robert S. 19, 24, 46
  Robt. S. 25, 51
Gillispie, Geo. 66
  James 17
  John 9
Ginkins, Elish (also see Elisha
    Ginkins) 39
  Elisha (also see Elish Ginkins)
    39
  Nancy 38
Gisley, Sam'l (also see Grigsby)
    23
Gist, Nathaniel 71
Givens, Crisey 51
  John 12
  Nancy 4, 31
Glasgow, James (Jr.) 21
Glass, Jane 41
  Robert 54
  Sally 18
Goddard, Ann 27
  Henry 48
  Jesse 21, 27
  John 33

Goddard (cont.)
  Nathan 48
  Polly 30
  William 48
Goens, Wm. 64
Goforth, Elizabeth 60
Goldsby, Catherine 32
Good, Bertha 20
  Edward 20
  George 57
  Girvel 59
  Zelpe 30
Gooden, Michael 54
Goodman, Catherine 17
  John 47
  Wm. 60, 66, 68
Goodrich, Persis (Mrs.) 6
Goodwin, Jesse 5
  Overton 66
  Overton P. 62
  William 48
Gordan, Lewis 42
Gordon, Joshua 67
Gormany, Thomas 2
Gossage, Thomas 25
Gossett, Evaline 57
  Kiziah 67
Gowen, Mathew 16
  Nathan 15
Gowers, Able 18
  Ann 21
Gragg, Lyda 6
Graham, Joseph 17
  Peggy 67
Grammer, David 59
  James 46
  Polly 67
  Washington 59
Grant, John 54
Grantan, Rosy 37
Grason, Stacey 4
Gravely, Susan (also see McCulley) 46
Gravet, John 40
Gray, Peter 15
  Richard 41
Green, Austin 57
  Austin L. 70
  Betsey 70
  Bruce 25
  Enoch 54
  Famellia 59
  Francis 16
  George 33
  Jas. 9

Green (cont.)
  John 21
  Lucy 44
  Meshac 33
  Polly 23
  Samuel 15
  Theodorick 30
  Wiiliam 25, 28, 54
Greer, Anna Maria 11
  Jane 68
Gregsby, George 21
Gregory, F. H. 44
Grevat, Robert 30
Gresham, Nehimah 33
Griffine, William 72
Griffith, A. E. 28
  Isaac 57
  Mathew 8
  Thomas 8
  Thos. 8
Griffy, Polly 49
Grigg, Alexander 52
  Moses 57
Grigsby, George 19, 25
  Lutherate 57
  Samuel 17
  Sam'l (also see Gisley) 23
Grimley, Keziah (also see Grinsley) 62
Grinant, John (also see Grinatt and Grunant) 43
Grinatt, John (also see Grinant and Grunant) 43
Grinsley, Keziah (also see Grimley) 62
Grubb, Daniel 15
  Samuel 54
  William M. 67
Grunant, John (also see Grinant and Grinatt) 43
Grunnit, Hiram 57
Guffey, Nancy 50
Gunning, John (also see Gennings) 43
Gwin, William 61
Hacker, Betsey 24
  Joel 61
  Joseph 10
  Julius 9
Hackney, James 57
Hagerty, Sarah 9
Hagewood, Benjamin 21
Haggard, Alfred 15
  Harritt 54
  Nathanial 72

Haggard (cont.)
  Nathaniel 64
  Polly 53
  Samuel 12
  Sarah 51
  Sattira 69
  Susana 15
Haggart, James 10
  John 10
Haggert, James 11
Haggerty, Priscilla 2, 10
  Prissilla 2
Hagler, John 58
  Sarah 58
Hagwood, Benjamin 31
Hail, Robert 64
  William 35
Haile, Anna 47
Hale, John M. 35
  Mary 23
  William 40
Haley, Allen 38
  Betsey 16
  David 41
  Eliza 62
  James 72
  John 55, 61
  John C. 62
  Lucy 29
  Martha 30
Hall, Garrett 21
  Lennie 13
  Mariana 39
  Martin 10
  Nancy 10
  Samuel C. 7
  Thomas 46
  William 30, 51
  Wm. 50, 52
  Zachariah 39
Hamblet, Betsey 33
  William 33
Hamelton, John 64
  Malinda T. (also see Hamilton)
    44
  Polly 49
  Sarah 23
Hamilton, James 18
  John 41
  Malinda T. (also see Hamelton)
    44
Hamlet, William 35
Hampton, William 23
Hanes, James I. 41
Hanis, John (also see Haynis) 41

Hanison, Archillas 64
Hankins, Gilbert 12
  Hannah 57
  James (also see Hawkins) 1, 7,
    12, 28, 50
  John 11, 25, 36, 46
  Joseph 3, 5, 14, 16, 21, 30,
    37
  Polly 1, 53
  Preston 41
  Sallie 7
  Sally 7
  Sarah 45
  Thomas 35
  William 12, 35
  Wright 17
Hannah, Drusilla 23
  Jane 38, 43
  Nancy 19
Hans (?), 43
Hanson, Delilah 1
Hapler, William 69
Harbert, John D. 54
Hardiman, Amelia 71
Hardin, Peggy 70
Hare, Daniel 4
Harker, Joseph 2
Harkins, Nancy 2
Harp, Allen 67
Harris, Annison (also see Ornson
    Harris) 48
  Archibald 28
  Barbara 22
  James (also see Harrison) 38,
    50
  Marian (also see Mariana Harris)
    45
  Mariana (also see Marian Harris)
    45
  Orison 52
  Ornson, also see Annison Harris)
    48
  Sally (also see Harvey) 22
  Samuel 25
  Susanna 52
  Thomas F. 45
Harrison, ? 12
  Archilla L. 57
  Elender 10
  James (also see Harris) 38, 57
  Jane 34
  John 12, 17, 29
Hart, Albert (also see Hurt) 33
  Eli 18
  Elizabeth 59

Hart (cont.)
  Gillington 61
  Henry 23
  John 11
  Patsey 24
  Polly 29
  Sawyer 27
Hartley, Elizabeth 32
  Patrick 70
  Pheby 49
  Rebecca 22
Harvey, John 46
  Jonathan 7, 14, 31, 34
  Lucy 17
  Marmaduke 17
  Matilda 51
  Robert 16
  Sally (also see Harris) 21, 22
  Samuel 46
  Thomas 9
  William 8, 40, 46
Harwick, William 21
Harwood, Elijah 57
Haskins, Betsy 38
  James 2
  John 50
  Nancy 43
  William 12
Hassler, Mahala 65
  Wm. 65
Haster, John (also see Hostler) 41
Hastler, Daniel 12
  Emily (also see Hostler) 53
Hatfield, Ciely 33
Hatley, Phebe 37
Haust (?), Abraham 61
Hawkins, James (also see Hankins) 28
  John 18.
  Susanah 4
  William 25
Hawks, Elizabeth 25, 33, 48
Hayewood, Benjamin 25
Haynes, Henry 8
  Isaac 70
  James P. 43
Haynis, John (also see Hanis) 41
Hays, Jeremiah R. 70
  Jesse 70
  Patsey 35
Hayse, Mary Jane 62
Haywood, Benjamin 18
Headrick, Peggy 21
  William 25
Heath, Elijah 64

Heath (cont.)
  Elizabeth 61
  Thomas 57
Hellunes, Eli 35
Helms, Jan 63
Hembree, Isaac 35
  Joel 51
  Joel B. 54
Henderson, Albert 25, 33, 48
  Michael 51
  Sally 39
  Washington 29
Hendreck, John 30
Hendrick, Jacob (F?) (also see Kindrick) 38
Hendrix, (Squire) 13
  Jonathan 35
  Morgan 21
Henley, Ruthy 4
  William 61
Henry, Ezekiel 7
  George 28
  Hannah 7
  Joseph 30
  Vinet 23
Hensley, Benjamin 43
  James 33
  Joseph B. 54
  Margaret 66
Henson, Elizabeth 59
  Jeremiah 4
  Jonathan 46, 59
Herbert, Scyntha 30
Hester, Abner 64
  Robert 59
Hewett, Robert 11
Hewitt, Anthony 27
Hickey, Charles 12
  Preston 6, 9
Hicks, Absolem 43
  Betsey 17
  Daniel 50
  James F. 59
  Mary 56
  Patsey 26
Hide, Hiram 17
Hiden, Elizabeth 46
Hider, Elizabeth 41
Higgins, Daniel 42
  Joseph 62
Highton, Lilly 36
  May Ann 65
  Patsey 31
Hightower, Patsy 38
Hill, Allen 22

Huff, Hannah H. 54
   Phillip 38
   Polly 44
   William 50
   William I. 58
Huffine, Daniel 38
   Ephraim 67
Huffman, Elizabeth 47
Hughes, John 3
   Polly (also see Hughlin) 34
Hughlin, Polly (also see Hughes) 34
Hughs, Abraham 58
   Elvira 58
   William 50
Hulsey, Mary 63
Humphreys, James 25
Hunds, Abigal 33
Hunt, James 13, 35
   John 2
   Sarah Ann 56
   Tarlton 18
Hunter, Lucinda 29
   Polly 37
Hurst, James 46
Hurt, Albert (also see Hart) 33, 48
   Nancy 33
Huse, Stephen 33
Husett, Jinny 9
Husk, John 6
Husong, William 64
Hutchison, Samuel 50
Hutson, Levina 58
   William 54, 70
Hyden, Anderson 43
Hynson, Jeremiah 4, 6
Hyten, Anderson (also see Andrew Hyten) 50
   Andrew (also see Anderson Hyten) 50
   Mary Ann 50
Ingleton, John 30
Ingram, David 33
   Gastand 33
   Hanover 67
   Peggy 48
   Sally 30
   Sanford 35
Inness, William (also see Eness or Enoss) 33
Ireland, Jinny 27
Irick, Uriah 43
Irvin, Betsey 14
   Rachel 17

Irwin, Byrd 28
   George 30
   James 54
   Rebeckah 25
   Sally 18
Isely, George 49, 51, 62
Isham, Charles 23
   Henry 23
   James 72
   Katy (also see Ditian) 47
Isly, George 46
Isreal, Rebecca 47
Ives, Thomas 57, 67
Jackson, Abel 37, 62
   Churchwell 59
   Isiah 25
   John 12, 26
   Josiah 31, 59
   Levi 67
   Patsey 17
   Polly 20
   Susan F. 72
Jakewish, Gabriel 50
James, Cory A. 46
   Henry 70
   J. A. 54
   James 4, 59
   Mahala 60
   Malinda 64
   Polly 55
   William 67
Jaquis, John 50
Jarralt, Nathaniel 44
Jeans, Mary 14
Jenkins, Henry 50
   Lucinda 47
Jent, Sinthy (also see Juet) 47
   William 24
Jinkins, Elizabeth 27
   John 57
   Polly 60
   Sally 38
John, Ezekeil 67
Johnson, Berry 72
   Betsey 45
   Calvin 11
   Charity 36
   Ebenezer (also see Johnston) 46, 54
   Francis J. 72
   Gains 3
   Harriet G. 67
   Hiriam 42
   Isaac 37, 49
   James 50, 57

Longaire, Ann 21
Longbottom, Elijah 50
Looney, Moses 21
Loony, Elizabeth 48
  Milly 19
  Preston 48
Lore, Joseph N. 67
Loutten, Jacob (also see Lacetter)
  30
Love, Hezekiah 28, 68
  John M. 19
  Richard H. 8
  Robert 44, 67
Lovelace, Ann 53
  Polly 67
  Wm. 57
Lovelass, William 48
Loveless, William 46
  Zadak 46
Lovely, William L. 6
Low, Isaac L. 57
  Jesse 59
  Jesse M. 56
Lowe, Jesse 38
  Jesse M. 60
  Thomas 57
Lower, Betsey 36
  George W. 70
  Jacob (also see Tower) 68
  Julie Ann 58
  Lucy 28
  Michael 58
  Roaanna (?) 23
Lowery, Jacob 67
  John 2
Loyd, John 12, 17, 20, 24, 28, 33,
  44
Luckjon, Mile (also see Tuckson)
  44
Luellen, Nancy 68
Luster, Elizabeth 1, 4
  James 4
  John 4
  Jonathan 36
  William 2
Luten, Wiley 41
Luttrell, Edw. 59
  Edward 11
  Elizabeth 62
  Katherine 46
  Locky 66
  Martin 60
  Mason 11
  Peggy 2
  Polly B. 62

Luttrell (cont.)
  Sarah 68
  Silas 14
Lyle, Elizabeth 60
  Henry 50
  Jenny 12
  Joseph 38
  L. Addison 62
  Patsey 66
  Priscilla 8
  Robert 12, 42, 66
  Sally 12, 37
Lyles, David 16, 60
  Fannie 6
  Fanny 4
  Rebecca 56
  Robert 6
  William (also see Syler) 36
Lynn, James 67, 70
Lyon, Letitia 8
  William 7, 8
Lyons, William 42
Lyttle, Luke 23
McAlester, William 38
McAnally, Mary Ann 26
  Nancy 22
McAnelly, Bartlet 17
McBath, (?) 68
  Mary 68
McCabb, James W. 36
McCabe, Nancy 24, 25
  Patsey 29
McCain, Gracy 37
  Peggy 10
McCall, Nancy 52
  Samuel 9, 10
  Tolbut 60
McCally, William 48
McCampbell, James 23
McCarmack, Samuel 52
McCarroll, John 54
  Synthea 56
McCarty, William 19
McCastand, Harmon 66
McCawl, Eliza H. (also see McCowl)
  42
McChaney, William 64
  Wm. 65
McChany, Wm. C. (also see McKamey)
  26
McClelan, Elizabeth 42
McClellan, Abraham 1, 4, 23
  Daniel 8
  John 21
  Joseph (also see McClenchan) 23

McClellan, Samuel 23
  Wm. 21
McClenchan, Joseph (also see
    McClellan) 23
McClesta, John 54
McClintock, James 9
McCloud, Jesse 51
McClure, Isabella 28
McCollom, Ally 41
McCollum, Polly 33
McComb, Jinny 10
  Polly 31
McConnell, (?) 19
  William 26
McCord, John 2
McCorkle, Rachel 12
McCormick, Clayton 28
  John 57
  Mary 31
McCowan, Charity 61
McCowin, Wm. M. 40
McCowl, Eliza H. (also see McCawl)
    42
McCown, Sally 21
McCoy, Mary 5
McCrary, Polly 8
McCrery, Barbary 44
McCulley, Susan (also see Gravely)
    46
McCullock, Alexander 26
  Andrew 68, 69
McCullough, Alexander 55
  Andrew 64
  J. W. 72
  James 5
McDaniel, Abner 48
  Alexander 36
  Caleb (also see McDonald) 26
  Charity 28
  Daniel 5
  David (also see McDonald) 23, 26
  Jacob 62
  John 56
  Nelly 19
  William 41
McDonald, Caleb (also see McDaniel)
    26
  David (also see McDaniel) 26
  Elizabeth 8
  Peggy 14
McDuffee, Anguish 72
  Elizabeth 72
McDuffy, Catherine 33
  John 70
McElwee, John 4

McElwee (cont.)
  Julia 67
  Mary 70
  Nancy 26
  Sarah 39
  Thomas 72
McEwen, Eliza M. E. 40
  John 25
  Mathew P. 72
  William L. 58
  William M. 58
McEwin, Eliza M. E. 41
  John 7, 25, 60
  John C. 60
  N. 66
  Robt. N. 70
McFail, Hugh 21
McFarland, Arthur (also see
    McForland) 46
McForland, Arthur (also see
    McFarland) 46
McGhee, Bartly 2
McGill, David 8
  James 8
McGomery, S. 39
McGuire, Thomas 30
McHenry, Robert 31, 38
McIntire, Archibald 61
  Elizabeth 28, 48
  James 60
  Jane 68
  John 64
  Mary Kate 61
McIntirf, Manuel 33
McKain, James 3
  Polly 34
  William 38, 39
McKamey, Anna 29
  Elizabeth 17
  James 19
  Margaret 71
  Nancy 11
  William 20, 31, 39
  William N. 71
  Wm. 57
  Wm. C. (also see McChaney)
    26, 52, 57
McKamy, Anna 37
  C. 35
  Isabella 21, 24
  John 8, 37
  William 18
  William C. 19
  Wm. 10, 29
  Wm. C. 18, 20, 24

McKane, Edward 25
  John 54
  Peter 60
McKaney, William 11
McKidy, Elinor 23
McKinney, Alexander 8
  Augustus 12
  Dicy 47
  Elizabeth 32
  Jesse 51
  John 2
  Polly 46
  Rebecca 54
  Sarah C. 55
  Syntha Ann 47
  Thomas 3, 36
  William 2, 3, 47
  Wm. C. 55
McKinnie, Priscilla 18
  Reuben 12
McKinny, Nancy 66, 70
  Samuel 5
McKnight, Backster 41
McLain, Thomas 65
McLure, David 62
  John 62
McMead, William 33
McMeans, Isaac 13
McMillan, Flora 58
McMinn, Joseph 19
  Margaret T. 43
McMullin, Becky 70
  James 8, 12
  Jane 56
  Nancy 25, 43
  Rebecca 8
  Samuel 8, 26
  Sarah 64
  Thomas 15, 48
McNabb, Andrew 60
  Eli 31
  George 67
  Peggy 18
  Polly 50
  Sarah 19
  Thomas 31
McNair, James 12
McNairy, John 3
McNatt, Nathan 31
McNight, Polly 40
McNite, Polly 57
McNutt, Caty 8
  James 5, 6
  John 15, 26, 51
  Rebecca 15

McNutt (cont.)
  Robert 41
  Thomas 41
  William 5, 6, 41
  Wm. 21
  Zilphia 21
McPherson, Alexander 42
  Barto- 13, 23
  Elener 24
  Elinor 30
  Elizabeth 20
  Hannah 13
  Hugh L. W. 62
  Isaac 18
  James 33
  Jesse 33
  Jinny 27
  John 55
  Joseph 21
  Margaret 38, 42
  Mary 55
  Nancy 13
  Peggy 19
  Richard 33
  Spencer 33
  Susanah 72
  William 43
  Wm. 61
McReynolds, Wm. 70
McRoberts, John 23
McVay, Peggy (also see McVey) 25
McVey, Peggy (also see McVay) 25
Maberry, Fanny 63
Maddon, John 42
Maddox, William 41
Maddy, Sarah 65
Maden, William T. 41
Magee, Silas M. 48
Magill, Charles 64
  James 48
  John 62
  Robert 60, 62, 67
  William 57
Mahaffee, John 64
Mahan, Alex 4
  Alexander 3, 4
  Ethelinda 55
  Margaret 33
  Moses 17
  Nancy 5
  Pheby 4
  Robert 3
Mainard, Jesse 36
Majors, Abner 8
  William 64

Moore (cont.)
   Majory 22
   Mary 27
   Morris 5
   Nancy 68
   Peggy 19
   Polly 10
   Robert 31
   Sally 7
   Samuel 44
   Thomas 5, 9, 11
Moorehead, Richard 39, 65
Moorman, Rudolph 23, 27, 28
More, Henry 39
Morefield, George 19
Moreman, Rudolph 23
Morgan, Betsey (also see Patsey
    Morgan) 29, 40
   Edward T. 31
   Ellinor 38
   Gideon 30, 31
   James 65
   John 11, 65
   Milly 9
   Nancy 34
   Patsey (also see Betsey Morgan)
    29
   William 3
Morris, Israel 49
   James 3
   Jenny 26
   Nancy 45
   Oliver 14
   Peggy 58
   Robert 60
   Stephen 5, 6
Morrison, John B. 45
Morrow, James 11
Moses, John 28
Moss, Joseph 33, 65
Mosse, Anna 27
Moton, John 11
Mounds, John 68
Mount, Julius 41
Mulky, Phemy 20
Mullins, Ann 69
   B. L. 44
   Betsey 65
   Susan 69
Mund, Betsey 12
Munds, Nelson 70
Mungor, Polly 47
Murphy, Sarah 52
Murrah, John 34
Murray, E. D. 63

Murray (cont.)
   Rachel 37
Murrey, C. L. 62
   Rachel 35
Musgrove, Edward 23
   William 41
Nail, Alexander 34, 58
   Andrew 22, 28
   James 5, 8
   John 31, 55
   Joseph 22
   Mariam 44
   Mathew 8
   Monann 44
   Nancy 8, 22
   Synthia 48
   William 28, 70
Nance, Patsey 28
Napier, Thomas 55, 70
Narramore, Wade 68
Nave, Samuel 38
Neal, John 10
   Lucinda 8
Neil (?), Olly 66
   William 72
Neilson, William D, 15
Neiper, James 68
Nelson, John E. 17, 41, 57
   Martin 6, 8
   Mary 3
   Mathew 7, 9
   Pulaski 39
   Thomas 41
Nesmith, Alexander 32, 34
   John 39
   Thomas 51
New, William 41
Newman, Charity 54
   Conrad 22
   Elizabeth 33
   Henry 33
   Nimrod 65, 71
   Sarah 55
Newport, Calvin 62
Nexmith, Alex 36
Nichols, John 10
   Louisa 59
Nicholson, Sarah 59, 62
Nichone (?), William 31
Nickland, William 38
Niper, Caswell Allen 71
Nipp, Samuel 11
Nipper, James 26
Noble, James 8
   Robert 5, 53

Sawyer (cont.)
  Larkin 15
Scabrough, James 72
Scarborough, George 58
Scarbrough, Eliza 69
  Prudence 67
Scavitart, William 47
Scisco, Susana 36
Scott, Catherine 49
  Eliza 13
  Jane 2, 26
  John 19, 41
  Nancy 57
  Thomas 23
  William 47
Scrivner, David 10, 15, 21
Scrogains, Jacob 42
Seal, James 59
Seales, Joseph 42
Seaton, Elizabeth 14
Selbe, John 29, 34
  Samuel 26, 37
  William 26, 34
Self, Daniel 7, 8
  Henry 7
  Levi 7
  Winefred 8
Sellers, Isaac 34
  Isiah 60
  Michael 29
  Polly 72
  William 55
Selvadge, Emily 49
  Michael 49
Selvage, George 24
  Hannah 53
  John 52
  Michael 51
  Michael K. 69
  Willia- 53
Selvidge, Jane 38
  M. K. 51
Selvy, Susan (also see Silvay) 47
Senter, Tandy 15
Sevier, E. G. 67
  Eldridge G. 47
  Samuel 52
Sewell, Wm. 62
Sexton, Elizabeth 18
  Jane 24
  Sally 23
  William (also see Sutian) 42
Shackleford, William 71
  Zachariah 65
Shadden, Rebecca 16

Shadden (cont.)
  Robert 16
  Sucky 1
Shaddrick, Rebecca 64
Shadrick, Joseph (also see
    Shadwick) 47
  Rebecca (also see Shadwick) 38
  Stephen 22
Shadwick, Joseph (also see
    Shadrick) 47
  Rebecca (also see Shadrick) 38
  Sarah 72
Shafer, Abraham 6
  Abraham K. 8, 9
Shanan, Patsey (also see Patty
    Shanan) 43
  Patty (also see Patsey Shanan)
    43
Shaifer, Abraham 10
Shain, Ann (also see Shaw) 32
Shakeford, David 22
Shannan, Jonathan 72
Sharkey, Betsey 2
Sharky, Polly 2
Sharp, Beany 44
  Jean 3
  John 36
  John A. 70, 71
  Margaret 27
  Polly 22
  Sally 10, 17, 45
Sharrin, Patsey 43
Shaw, Amy 69
  Ann (also see Shain) 32
  David, 24
Shell, John 60
  Lucinda 48
  Jeremiah 14
Shelton, Eli 16
  Mathew 56
Shephard, Louisa 3, 15
Sherold, Jesse 5
  Mattie 5
Sherrell, Elizabeth 46
  Jesse 6, 7
  Patsy 3
Sherrill, William 2
Shields, Anna 21
  Benjamin 13
  John (also see Shirley) 24, 51,
    68
  John S. 58
  Phebe 17
Shinalt, Isaac 4
Shirley, John (also see Shields) 24

109

Spraggins, Sally 70
Sprall, Celly 46
Spralt, John 55
Springston, Edward 6
Stafford, Noah 6
  Thomas 3
Staples, Abner 24
  Andrew 39
  John M. 24
  Mary 71
Starke, Fanny 2
Starkey, Joseph 16
Starks, Betsey 19
Staton, Polly 37
Stean, Nancy 16
Steane, William (also see Sloane)
  26
Steel, Lucy 47
Steen, William 58
Stegall, Henry 68
  Richard 65
Stennett, Mahaley Jane 72
Stephens, (?) 34
  Charles 19
  George 10, 22
  Patsey 18
  Philip 21, 22, 33, 50
  Rufus 60
  Shadrick 18
Stephenson, Anne 44
  James 49, 52
  Millican 72
  Thomas 14
Stevins, Rufus M. 62
Steward, Sarah (also see Stewart)
  32
Stewart, David 2
  Edward 15, 24
  George 64
  Hessy 21
  Jane 43
  John 31
  Mary Eleanor 68
  Rachel 26
  Sally 56
  Sarah (also see Steward) 32
  William 21
Stinson, Eliza M. 7
Stivers, Samuel 29
Stockton, Martha 58
  Thomas 60
  Willis 20, 55
Stogdon, Smith 60
Stone, Caty 7
  James 63, 68

Stone (cont.)
  Madison 52
  Manoah 68
  Matilda 59
  Robert (also see Stout) 28
  Sarah 3
Stonecipher, Peggy 9
Stonecypher, Rhoda 12
Stormen, Jefferson 55
Stout, Abraham 12, 14
  George W. 68
  Milly 30, 37, 42
  Moses 30
  Nancy 23
  Robert (also see Stone or
    Stow) 28, 42, 50
  Ruth 11
  Sally 34
  Samuel 9, 10, 13, 14, 18, 20
  Thomas 29
Stover, Eliza 10
Stow, John 19
  Robert (also see Stout) 49, 50
  Samuel 19
  Solomon 29, 36, 47
Strain, Angeline 61
Straisner, Michael 7
Strange, Martin 68
Strong, Augustus 3, 15
Stubb, Jenny 7
  John 31, 44
Stubbs, Asha 34
  Claibourn 63
  Everett 14
  John 44
  Louis 12
  Mahala 69
  Mary Ann (also see Suttle) 58
  Nancy 28
  Penelope 61
Stukesberry, Joseph 65
Stults, Anna 55
  Betsey 30
  James 29
  John 30
  Penelphia (also see Penolpina
    Stults) 52
  Penolpina (also see Penelphia
    Stults) 52
Stultz, Nancy (also see Shultz)
  24
Sturges, Wentley 44
Sturgess, Wesley 52
  Westley 55
Sturgis, Westley 48

Suddath, Benjamin 47
 Francis 61
 John 52
 Margaret E. 61
 Richard S. 61
Suel, Ann 59
Sullens, Josiah 57
Sullin, Henry (also see Sutter)
 34
Sullins, Jacob 59
 Larkin 52
Sullivan, Winney 2
Summers, Sally 2
Sumpter, Lewis M. 58
Suthard, William 67
Sutherland, Alen 56
Sutian, William (also see Sexton)
 42
Sutter, Henry (also see Sullin)
 34
Suttle, Mary Ann (also see Stubbs)
 58
Sutton, Amy 30
 Betsey 27, 34
 Betsy 47
 Betty 35
 James 27
 Jane (also see June Sutton) 9
 John 52
 June (also see Jane Sutton) 9
 Louis 47
 William 37
Swafford, William 72
Swan, Samuel 26
 Thos. B. 42
Sweazea, Charles 7
 Richard 7
Sweny, Edward 2
Sweza, Nancy 7
Sylar, Elizabeth 58
Syler, Mary M. 63
 William (also see Lyles) 36
Sylor, Peter (also see Tyler) 44
Talbot, Nancy 16
Talent, Nancy 17
Taliaferro, Benj. 42
 John 39
TalRichard H. (also see Talifaro)
 37
Talifaro, Richard H. (also see
 Taliaferro) 37
Taliferro, Betsey 58
Tallant, Barbara 60
 Sarah 44
 Sherod A. 42

Talliaferro, Richard H. 47, 52
Talliferro, Hatty 72
Tally, John H. 68
 Kinchen 63
Tammins (?), John 41
Tanner, Benjamine 55
 Burwele 37
 Thomas 37
Tarbour, Zylphey 2
Tarner, Elizabeth 72
Tate, Isaac 34, 61
 Peggy 32
 Rebecca 50
Taylor, Catherine 4
 Charlott 56
 Clarka 32
 Dennis 63
 E. D. 33
 Etheldred 29
 Etheldrid 13
 Ethelridge 31
 Eveline 45
 James 49
 Jane 44, 48
 John 26, 32, 52
 Lahida 46
 Michael 36
 Patsey 33
 Peggy 7
 Sarah 58
 Thomas 26
 William 22
Tedder, John 26
 Nancy 25
Tedier, James (also see John
 Tedier) 31
 John (also see James Tedier)
 31
Temple, James H. 39
Tennor, Mary 44
Tenor, Adam 55
Terry, Jesse 18
 Jessy 28
 John C. 68
 Jonah 40
 Martha 28
 Moly 40
 Samuel 45
Thacker, John 13
 Samuel 9
 Umphrey 61
 William 15
Thomas, Andrew 22
 Betsy 3
 David 12

113

Underwood, Abner 14
  Baldwin 27, 49
  Elvira 64
  Ethalinda 55, 70
  James H. 52
  John 34
  Jonathan 37, 44
  Narcissa 55
  Nimrod 72
  Polly 38
  Thomas J. 68
  William 64, 68
  Wm. 52
Upshaw, Peter 22
Upton, Thomas 5
Uteley, Jacob 47
  William 24
Utley, Howard 31
Vance, Daniel (also see Vann) 31
Vandegrift, Alla 61
Vann, Daniel (also see Vance) 31
  Vann, John 69
Varner, Adam 69
  David 64
  Polly 64
Vaughn, A. P. 61
  Ann 56
  Celia 17
  George 8
  Malinda 62
  Mary 66
  Nancy 20
  Nicey 16
  Polly 62
  Sally 15
  William 19
Vess, James J. (also see Vest) 42
Vest, James J. (also see Vess) 42
Vickey, Chryleena 24
Vincent, John 27
Voiles, Levi 69
Waddy, Samuel 7, 8, 34
Wade, David M. 58
Wake, Sarah 64
Wakefield, James 61
Walker, (?) 31
  Audley 17
  Audley P. 31
  Buckner 10
  Catherine 35
  Charles 47
  Edward 3
  Elenor 71
  Elinor 45
  Elizabeth 45

Walker (cont.)
  Ephraim 2, 3
  Finney Letterson 8
  John 3, 7, 47, 61
  Joseph 2
  Malinda 51
  Milly 54
  Peggy 3
  Rebecka 12
  Sally 2
  Sam'l S. 24
  Samuel 8, 29, 45
  Samuel R. 17
  Samuel S. 36
  Suckie (also see Cherokees) 10
  Thomas 18, 55
  Wiley 11
  William 45
  William F. 58
  William P. 53
Wallace, John 42
  Sarah 19
  William 19
Waller, Anna W. 57
  Carr 42
  Edward 6
  Enid 4
  John B. 39, 42
  Mary 68
  William 59, 63
Wallis, Thomas 52
Ward, Jane 39, 44
  Nancy 54
  Nicholas 49
Warden, David 10
Warding, David 10
Waren, Elizabeth 50
  Jacob 35, 63
  James W. 51
  John 14
  Nancy 35
  Polly 48
Warren, Edmond (also see Edward
    Warren) 17
  Edward (also see Edmond Warren)
    17
  Elmira 56
  Jacob 11, 36
  James 11
  Nancy 19
  Sally 17
  William 71
Waten, Jesse 27
Waters, Abner 13
Watson, Amy 31

Watson (cont.)
  John 13
  Jane K. 70
  Leander 58
  Martin 55
  Mary Ann 59
  Nathan 47
  Samuel 24
Watt, Absolom (also see West) 44
  Peggy 61
  Richard 72
Wear, Gilbert 61
  Hugh 2
  John 2
  Mary 2
Wearing, John 7
Webb, David 8
  Elizabeth 63
  Jane 54
  John 10
  Judy 31
  Levicy 42
  Lucy 53
  Martin 63
  Nancy 49
Webster, David 26
Weece, Abraham (also see Weese) 69
Weese, Abraham (also see Weece) 69
  Betsey 29
  George 68
  John 29, 47
  Landon 66
  Nancy 55
  Polly 45, 71
  Rebecca 65
  Sam'l 65
  Samuel 69
  Sarah (also see Weiss) 41
  Solomon 69
  William 44, 55, 69, 72
  William S. 55
Weir, Andrew 14
  Mary 14
Weiss, Sarah (also see Weese) 41
Welhite, Isaac (also see Wilhite) 52
Wells, Eliza 52
  Emma Middleton 1
  James 22
  Ludy 45
Wesse, Abraham 61
West, Absolom (also see Watt) 44
  Green 56

West (cont.)
  Jane 67
  Jesse 29
  John 20, 22, 52, 63, 66, 69
  Mariah 65, 71
  Nancy 50
  Nicholas 20
  Patsey 28
  Peggy 46
  Polly 25, 62
  Reuben 56
  Ruben 50
  Sally 40, 66
  Sarah 30
  Stephen 42, 49, 51
  Susan 66
  Susanna 30
  William 62
Westbrook, Amanda 52
  Champain 52
Wester, Amanda J. 69
  Daniel 29, 31, 47, 60, 64
  Edy 44
  Elizabeth 1, 15
  Polly 31
  Rachel P. 64
  William 47
Westmoreland, Ruth 28
Whalan, William 63
Wheat, Elizabeth 39
  George W. 5
  Henderson 71
  John 39
  Lear (also see Levi Wheat) 47
  Levi (also see Lear Wheat) 26, 33, 39, 46, 47
  Sally 46
White, Albina Minsco 22
  Allen 57
  Benj. J. 18
  Benjamin C. 25
  Betsy 13
  Bloomer 61
  Calvin 20
  Charles 13, 26, 33
  David 42
  Elizabeth 47
  George 13
  Harvey 49
  Hugh 3
  John 8, 61
  Joseph 42
  Lem 5
  Luther 24, 47
  Lyda 21

White (cont.)
  Margaret 27
  Mary 3
  Moses 58
  Peggy 4
  Rebecah 23
  Rebecca 23
  Rebecca W. 32
  Robert 8
  Sally 6
  Sarah 57
  William 4, 6, 24
Whith, Eany 20
Whittenburg, Abraham 52
  Benj. 52
Whittenburger, Benjamin 29
  Susana 20
Whitworth, Thomas 6
Wiatte, Dillid 55
Widener, Lewis 8
Wiggins, Benjamine 69
  Mary Jane 60
Wiggons, Ann 44
Wilcocks, Angeline 50
Wilcox, Sarah 61
Wiley, Henry 51, 61
  Henry H. 52, 63
  Jane 43
  John 54
  Nancy 51
  Patsey 20
Wilhite, Comfort 64
  Isaac (also see Welhite) 52
  Sally 54
Wilkerson, Ann 20
  Claiborn 65
  Eliza 46
  James 31
  John 15
  Samuel 7, 10
  Uriah 20
Wilkey, Roger 65, 71
Wilkins, Henry 37
  Solomon 39
Wilkinson, James 14
  William 37
Willaism, Susanna 22
Willett, Enoch 71
  James 5, 61, 70
  Jas, 3
  Nathaniel 52, 71
  Sarah (also see Sera Willett) 5
  Sera (also see Sarah Willett) 5
  Thos. G. 52
  William 3

William, Elisha 22
Williams, Amanda 35
  Amelia 35
  Benjamin 18
  Elizabeth 72
  Frances Jane 53
  Harriet 22
  Henrietta 8
  James G. 21, 22, 23
  John 19, 72
  John E. 71
  Jonathan 3
  Joseph 58
  Judah 61
  Lucinda 27
  Martin 72
  Mary 38, 57, 64
  Mathew 42
  Matthews 35
  Nancy 19, 47
  Parmelia (also see Permelia
    Williams) 41
  Permelia (also see Parmelia
    Williams) 41
  Polly (also see Woolsey) 31, 58
  Ruben 23, 27
  Sally 45
  Samuel 2, 13
  Sterling 31
  Tabitha 69
  Thomas 48, 56
  Thos. 32
  William 31, 38, 56
Williamson, Elisha 11, 24, 63
  John 64
  Nellie 24
  James 65
Willis, Andrew J. 61
  Eliza 36
  Frances M. 49
Wilmot, James 56
Wilson, Amos 65
  Elizabeth 7
  Emmey 5
  John 49, 52, 60
  John M. 27
  Peter 32
  Robert 69
  Samuel 20
  William 6, 32
Windle, John 37
Winegar, William 11
Wingener, Peter 8
Winten, Betsey 39
  Bobby 72

116

www.ingramcontent.com/pod-product-compliance
Lightning Source LLC
Chambersburg PA
CBHW071136280326
41935CB00010B/1245